Good News for KIDS

Series B

52 GOSPEL TALKS

Marti Beuschlein
Donna Bobb
Patsy List
Eileen Ritter

CPH
SAINT LOUIS

Copyright © 1996 Concordia Publishing House
3558 S. Jefferson Avenue, St. Louis, MO 63118-3968
Manufactured in the United States of America

Library of Congress Cataloging-in-Publication Data

Good news for kids : 52 Gospel talks / Elizabeth Friedrich ... [et al.].
    p.   cm.
   Contents: [1] Series A & B
   ISBN 0-570-04854-0 (Series B) :
   1. Bible—Liturgical lessons, English. 2. Christian education of children.
I. Friedrich, Elizabeth, 1949-
BS2565.G66   1995
252'.53—dc20   95-5762

---

1 2 3 4 5 6 7 8 9 10   05 04 03 02 01 00 99 98 97 96

Contents

Window Watcher

FIRST SUNDAY IN ADVENT: Mark 13:33–37

Text: "Be on guard! Be alert! You do not know when that time will come. … What I say to you, I say to everyone: 'Watch!' " *Mark 13:33, 37*

Teaching aids: A window frame large enough to look through cut from poster board; a Bible.

Gospel truth: Jesus promised that He would return to us. The Holy Spirit helps us to watch and be faithful.

Watching and waiting for someone we love can be hard. When Bethany turned five years old, her parents promised her a birthday party. She was very excited. Bethany helped her parents get ready for the special party. They cleaned the house. They planned some favorite games to play. They even baked a delicious cake with chocolate frosting.

As Bethany's mother put the cake on the table, she realized that she didn't have any birthday candles for it. "We'll need candles for Bethany to blow out," she said. "I'll go to the store and get some."

Bethany didn't want her mother to leave, but it would be nice to have five candles to blow out. So Bethany waited— and waited—and watched out the window. *Hold up the window each time she looks out.* She helped her daddy set the table. And she looked out the window. She put a napkin beside each plate. And she looked out the window. She wanted to go out to play, but her mother had told her to stay inside so she wouldn't get dirty. So she stayed inside and— Bethany waited—and waited—and she watched out the window.

Finally she could see her mother coming. Bethany was

so excited. When her mother came through the door, Bethany gave her a big hug. And the party began.

Watching and waiting for someone we love is hard. In the Bible Jesus tells us to watch for Him. He has promised that He will come to earth again. We can't watch out the window for Jesus to come, as Bethany did. But we can look in the Bible for good news about Jesus and His love for us. *Hold up the Bible.* And while we are waiting for Him to come, we have many things to do. God's Holy Spirit helps us learn more about our Savior and Friend, Jesus, by listening to stories in the Bible. We worship Him together with other Christians by singing songs and praising Him. We talk to Him in prayer whenever we want. And we also tell others about Jesus and the way He died on the cross for us to pay for our sins.

With Jesus' help we can watch and wait until He comes to take us to heaven just as He promised. And in heaven our most special party will begin.

Let's ask Jesus to help us watch and wait for Him. Please pray with me:

Prayer: Dear Jesus, we know that You have promised to come to earth again. Please help us watch and wait for You as we pray, praise, and worship You. Help us to tell others the good news of Your love. Amen.

Someone's Coming!

SECOND SUNDAY IN ADVENT: Mark 1:1–8

Text: "I will send My messenger ahead of You, who will prepare Your way—"… And so John came, baptizing in the desert region and preaching a baptism of repentance for the forgiveness of sins. *Mark 1:2, 4*

Teaching aid: Telephone

Gospel truth: God forgives our sins through the sacrifice of His Son.

Ring! Ring! It was the telephone. Patrick's dad picked up the phone. *Hold the phone as if you are listening.* He smiled and said, "That will be wonderful. We'll see you then. Goodbye."

Patrick couldn't wait to find out who was coming. "Patrick," said his dad. "Grandma is coming over in a little while!"

This was great news. Patrick loved to see his grandma. She had been away visiting friends for two weeks. It seemed like two years to Patrick. He couldn't wait to see Grandma again. But as Patrick thought about his grandma, he started to feel sad. He remembered the last time his grandma visited. Patrick hadn't been very nice to her. When she came, he was in the backyard, playing with his neighbor, Derrick. Patrick's father called him inside for a visit with Grandma. But Patrick didn't want to stop playing. He stamped his foot and said, "No! I'm busy!" He hurt his grandma's feelings. Now he felt very sad about doing that.

"Do you think Grandma will want to see me?" Patrick asked. "I wasn't very nice to her the last time she came. I wish I could tell her that I'm sorry."

"Let's call her now," said Daddy. *Hold up the phone.* Patrick called his grandmother. He told her how sorry he was about the way he behaved during her last visit. He asked her if she still wanted to see him. And Grandma said—YES! She still loved him, and she forgave him.

Before Jesus was born, God had some news to tell His people. He sent a man named John to tell the people to get ready. God was ready to send His Son, Jesus, to be the Savior. John told the people that the promised Savior was coming. The people were excited, just like Patrick. God's people had waited a long, long time for the Savior. But they had also done some wrong things. They had sinned. They wondered if God would still love them. John said the people should tell God how sorry they felt. That's called repentance. God promised to forgive His people, not because they said they were sorry, but because Jesus would take the punishment for their sins when He died on the cross. God still loved His people, just like Grandma loved Patrick.

Now the people were happy. Jesus, the Savior they had been waiting for, was coming. God still loved them. Hurray!

Can we ask Jesus to forgive the wrong things we do too? Sure we can. Do we need a telephone like Patrick did? No. We can talk to Jesus right now in prayer. And we know He will forgive us.

Prayer: Dear Jesus, thank You for hearing our prayer. Please forgive the wrong things we have done. Thank You for still loving us. Help us to live as Your children. Amen.

The Messenger

THIRD SUNDAY IN ADVENT:
John 1:6–8, 19–28

Text: There came a man who was sent from God; his name was John. He came as a witness to testify concerning that light, so that through Him all men might believe. *John 1:6–7*

Teaching aids: A newspaper; a simple invitation for each child to take home and give to a neighbor, friend, or relative, inviting them to Christmas worship services. (Be sure to list the specific days and times of the services.)

Gospel truth: God helps us share the Good News that Jesus came to be our Savior.

Open the newspaper as if to read it. I brought the newspaper with me today. It tells me what's happening. It announces when an important visitor will come to our city or when a meeting will be held or when a new store will open.

The newspaper is important to us. It has things we need to know. *Lay the newspaper aside.* What are some other ways we can find out what's happening? (*Let children respond—TV, radio, computer, friends, etc.*)

Long ago there were no newspapers or TVs or radios. If people wanted to find out the latest news, they would have to talk with other people. The news was passed on from person to person. So, if the ruler of a country had some important news for his people, he would send a messenger to announce it. The messenger would walk or ride a donkey through the villages and tell people the news. Sometimes it was good news, such as, "The governor will come and visit your village soon." And sometimes it wasn't good news at all: "You will need to pay more taxes."

One time God had a special message for His people on earth. He wanted all people to hear this message. So God sent a special messenger named John to announce the news. *Pretend to shout the message.* "Get ready! The Savior is coming!" John told the people.

This was wonderful news. The people had been waiting for Jesus for a very long time. They knew that God would keep His promise of sending a Savior, and now it was about to happen! Jesus was really coming! God's messenger, John, told them the good news.

God wants us to be His special messengers too. He helps us to tell people about His Son, Jesus. God wants them to know about Jesus' birthday, Christmas, and about Jesus' growing up to die for us and rise again. To whom could you tell this good news? *Acknowledge each answer.* God has promised to help us tell others this great news.

Hold up an invitation. I have a special invitation for each of you to take home today. It has some wonderful news on it. It tells about Jesus' birthday. You can give it to someone you know. It will tell them when our worship services are so they can come and celebrate Jesus' birthday with us here at church. Let's ask God to help us be His special messengers.

Prayer: Dear God, thank You for choosing us to be Your special messengers. Help us to share the good news of Jesus' birthday with the people we know. Help us to invite them to worship with us here at church. Amen.

Who, Me?

FOURTH SUNDAY IN ADVENT: Luke 1:26–38

Text: But the angel said to her, "Do not be afraid, Mary, you have found favor with God. You will be with child and give birth to a Son, and you are to give Him the name Jesus." ... "I am the Lord's servant," Mary answered. "May it be to me as you have said." Then the angel left her. *Luke 1:30–31, 38*

Teaching aids: None

Gospel truth: God chooses us to be His servants and guides us as we serve Him.

When Jamie got to school one day, his teacher said, "Jamie, you're our helper today." Jamie was surprised—and excited—and a little bit scared. Who, me? he thought. He wasn't sure that he could do all the jobs his teacher might ask him to do.

Have you ever been the class helper? What kind of jobs did you do? *Let children respond.* Could you do them? Were all of the jobs you did fun things? What if your teacher wanted you to clean out the smelly hamster cage? That would be a hard job, wouldn't it? It would be easier if you had someone to help you.

Long ago God sent His angel, Gabriel, to see a young woman named Mary. God wanted her to be His helper. The angel said to Mary, "You will be the mother of Jesus, God's Son." Mary was surprised—and excited—and a little bit scared. Maybe she thought, "Who, me?" like Jamie did. But God promised to help her, just as He helps us. And Mary said, "I am the Lord's servant." That means God's helper. Mary was happy that God had chosen her.

God asks us to be His helpers too. We are His chosen ones, like Mary. You might think, "Who, me? What can I do?" What are some ways you can be God's helpers? *(Offer an example or two to get the children started. Include: Be kind to one another. Tell others about Him. Worship and praise Him. Take care of His world. Help Mom and Dad, brothers and sisters. etc.)*

Those are wonderful ways to be God's servants—His helpers. Let's ask God to help us do them.

Prayer: Dear God, thank You for choosing us to be Your helpers. Help us to say, "I'll be the Lord's servant." Show us ways to do things for You. Amen.

The Great Promise Keeper

FIRST SUNDAY AFTER CHRISTMAS:
Luke 2:25–40

Text: It had been revealed to him (Simeon) by the Holy Spirit that he would not die before he had seen the Lord's Christ. … When the parents brought in the child Jesus to do for Him what the custom of the Law required, Simeon took Him in his arms and praised God. *Luke 2:26–28*

Teaching aids: A kitchen timer to be set longer than needed to indicate the passage of time. A small gift for each child such as a sticker, a plastic ring, or a piece of individually wrapped candy. Hide the gifts in a container or basket.

Gospel truth: God keeps all His promises, just as He kept His promise to send Jesus to be our Savior.

Do you know what a promise is? *Let children respond.* If someone promises to do something, it means they will really do it, right? Has your mom or dad ever promised to do something for you? What did they promise to do? *(Examples: Take you to the movies or shopping. Let you choose the restaurant for your family's night out. Let you sit in the front seat of the car or van.)* Did they keep their promises? *(If necessary, give an example of a time when an adult might have to break a promise.)* How does it make you feel if someone doesn't keep their promise?

Well, today I'm going to make you a promise. I'm going to set this timer. *Set timer and hold it up.* When it rings, I promise I will give each of you a special little gift. How does that promise make you feel? Excited? Happy? Is it a little hard to wait for the promise?

Long ago there was a man named Simeon. He was waiting too. God had promised to send His people a Savior. Simeon was waiting for that Savior. But God made another promise just to Simeon. God promised Simeon that he would live to see the Savior. Simeon was so excited. He would get to see God's Son. So Simeon waited and waited just like you are doing now.

When Simeon was an old man he was still waiting. He believed that God would keep His promise. One day when Simeon was at the temple, he saw Mary and Joseph come in. Mary was carrying baby Jesus. God let Simeon know that this baby was the promised Savior. Simeon took Jesus in his arms and praised God. He thanked God for keeping His promise and letting him see the newborn Savior.

People cannot always keep the promises they make. Things happen and get in the way of the promises. But we know that every promise God has made, He will keep. He is our great Promise Keeper. And He can even help us keep the promises we make. And best of all, He can help us forgive each other when we cannot keep our promises.

"Help" the timer ring. There's our timer. What was that supposed to mean? Right. I promised to give you each a special little gift when we heard it. You remembered my promise. You were patient waiters just like Simeon. *Distribute the gifts.* Hold your gifts in your hands as we talk to God together.

Prayer: Dear God, thank You for keeping all of Your promises. We especially thank You for keeping Your promise to send Jesus, our Savior. Help us to forgive each other when we don't keep the promises we make. And remind us of Your promise to take care of us each day. Amen.

Just Like Us

SECOND SUNDAY AFTER CHRISTMAS:
John 1:1–18

Text: The Word became flesh and made His dwelling among us. We have seen His glory, the glory of the One and Only, who came from the Father, full of grace and truth. *John 1:14*

Teaching aids: Pictures or actual items as follows: an apple, glass of water, pair of sandals, shirt, hammer, pillow, mirror; place objects in a bag or box.

Gospel truth: Jesus, true God and true man, became a real person to live and die for us.

I have a guessing game for you today. *Hold up bag or box.* In here I have several things that are needed by someone or something. I'll show you the things. You see if you can guess who or what needs all these things. *As you pull each item out, give it to one of the children to hold.* What is this? Who uses it? *Guide the children to the response: people.*

These are all things that people need and use. Let's look at each one again. *Ask the child with the apple to hold it up.* People need food like apples in order to live. Jesus needed food, too, when He lived here on earth. He was just like us. Where is the water? We all need water each day, don't we? Jesus needed water too. He was just like us. Jesus needed clothes and shoes like these. *Point to the items.* He was just like us. Jesus needed tools like this hammer too. He was a carpenter here on earth. He did work, just like us. Jesus needed a place to sleep here on earth. He often stayed with His friends. He was just like us. And Jesus needed people to love Him. *Show the children their faces in the mirror.* He was just like us.

Jesus was just like us. When He was tired, He had to rest. When He was hungry, He had to eat. When He stubbed His toe, it hurt, and He had to rub it—just like us. Jesus was born a real person just like us. He knows how we feel when we are hungry or sad or hurt. He has promised to be with us always and help us, whether we are tired or happy or lonely. He understands what it's like to be a real person.

But there was one difference between Jesus and us. Jesus never did anything wrong. He never sinned. He came to show us how to live as God's people should. He was perfect. And He came to die to take away the sins that we commit. Those are the wrong things that we do. Jesus forgives us and makes us happy again. He is really God and man.

Prayer: Dear Jesus, thank You for becoming a real person—just like us. Thank You for dying to take away our sins. Help us to live as Your forgiven children. And remind us that You are always with us to help us. Amen.

God's Own Child

THE BAPTISM OF OUR LORD: Mark 1:4–11

Text: At that time Jesus came from Nazareth in Galilee and was baptized by John in the Jordan. As Jesus was coming up out of the water, He saw heaven being torn open and the Spirit descending on Him like a dove. And a voice came from heaven: "You are My Son, whom I love; with You I am well pleased." *Mark 1:9–11*

Teaching aids: Water in the baptismal font, a small towel, a picture of a dove. (Use a symbol within your sanctuary if possible.)

Gospel truth: God claims us as His children in Baptism, through the forgiveness won by His Son.

Michael was in kindergarten. His class was getting ready for a special day. All of the parents were invited to visit the classroom. The children painted special pictures of animals to display for their parents. Michael did his very best job of painting a dog to show his parents. When the special day arrived, the parents walked around the room. They saw where the children kept their pencil boxes. They saw where the picture books were lined up on the shelf. And they saw the paintings of animals hanging on the bulletin board. Michael watched as his parents looked at each of the paintings. Then he heard his dad say, "This one is by my son, Michael. I'm very proud of him." Then his dad pointed to Michael. He smiled and said, "That's him over there." Michael came over and gave his dad a big hug.

Michael's dad wanted everyone to know that Michael was his son. Long ago God wanted His people to know that Jesus was His Son. Jesus came to a river where God's helper,

John, was baptizing people. The people watched as John baptized Jesus in the river. As Jesus was coming out of the water, God sent the Holy Spirit down from heaven. The Spirit looked like a bird called a dove. That picture of the dove reminds us of the Holy Spirit. *Point to such a picture.* Suddenly a voice came from heaven. It was God's voice. God said, "This is My Son, whom I love. I am very pleased with Him." The people watching knew then that Jesus was really God's Son. They knew that God loved His own dear Son very much.

God loves us very much too. That is why He gave us a special blessing called Baptism. Let's look at the baptismal font. *Gather the children near the font.* When you were baptized, your parents and sponsors brought you here. The pastor made the sign of the cross on your head and heart. He asked you if you believed in God the Father, the Son, and the Holy Spirit. Your sponsors answered yes for you. Then the pastor poured water on your head and said, "I baptize you in the name of the Father and of the Son and of the Holy Spirit." *Dip your hand in the water to show the children that real water was used.*

When you were baptized, God made you His own child. He put the love of Jesus in your heart. It's called your faith. As you grow, God helps your faith in Him grow too. Through Baptism you became a forgiven child of God. Because Jesus, God's Son, died to take your sins away, God calls you His own child too. He will always be near you and forgive your sins. He is happy that you are His own child.

Prayer: Dear God, thank You for Your gift of Baptism. Thank You for forgiving the many wrong things I do each day. Thank You for making me Your own dear child. In Jesus' name. Amen.

Follow the Leader

―――◆―――

SECOND SUNDAY AFTER THE EPIPHANY:
John 1:43–51

Text: The next day Jesus decided to leave for Galilee. Finding Philip, He said to him, "Follow Me." ... Philip found Nathanael and told him, "We have found the one Moses wrote about in the Law, and about whom the prophets also wrote—Jesus of Nazareth. ... Come and see." *John 1:43, 45–46*

Teaching aids: Two balloons with faces drawn on them. One balloon should be larger than the other. (Option: two puppets.)

Gospel truth: Jesus calls us to follow Him and helps us follow His example.

Hold up the smaller balloon puppet. This is Bryan. He's three years old. He likes to ride his tricycle, play in the sandbox, and build with blocks. But most of all, he likes to play Follow the Leader with his older brother, Robbie. *Hold up the larger balloon puppet.* When Robbie walks around the edge of the driveway, so does Bryan. When Robbie crawls under the picnic table, so does Bryan. When Robbie sits under the tree to rest, so does Bryan. The two boys have lots of fun—usually.

Sometimes, though, following Robbie is too hard for Bryan. Bryan isn't old enough or strong enough to keep up with Robbie all the time. For example, when Robbie climbed the hill behind their house, Bryan couldn't make it. Robbie was a good leader and a good brother. He came back to where Bryan was sitting. Robbie took his little brother's hand and helped him make it to the top. Bryan felt so happy to be there with Robbie. He gave Robbie a hug.

In today's Gospel lesson we hear that Jesus told a man named Philip to follow Him. Jesus didn't want to play Follow the Leader with Philip. Jesus wanted Philip to come and be with Him as He told people about God's love. Jesus wanted Philip to watch and learn from Him so Philip could be God's helper. By following Jesus' example, Philip would learn how a child of God lives.

Philip was so excited that he went to find Nathanael. He told him that Jesus, the promised Savior, wanted Philip to be one of His followers. Nathanael came to see Jesus and followed Him too.

Jesus calls us to follow Him, just as Philip and Nathanael did. He helps us to learn from His example. When we hear stories about Jesus from the Bible, we learn how to live as God's children.

Sometimes it's easy to follow Jesus. When we are worshiping here together with other Christians, it often seems easy to do what Jesus has told us to do. But sometimes it's hard to follow Jesus. When we want to do something and we know it's wrong, it's hard to stop. If your friends wanted you to go to a hockey game this morning instead of coming to church, it might be hard for you to come to worship.

Jesus has promised to help us when following Him gets too hard. If we are having trouble doing what Jesus wants us to do, we can pray and ask Him to help us. He will show us the right things to do in God's Word and help us to do them. He promises to forgive us when we don't follow Him. Jesus loves us. He is the best leader to follow. Even better than Robbie.

Prayer: Dear Jesus, thank You for calling us to follow You. Help us to learn how to live as God's children by following Your example. Help us when the following gets hard. And please forgive us when we make a wrong choice and don't follow You. Amen.

Going Fishing

THIRD SUNDAY AFTER THE EPIPHANY:
Mark 1:14–20

Text: As Jesus walked beside the Sea of Galilee, He saw Simon and his brother Andrew casting a net into the lake, for they were fishermen. "Come, follow Me," Jesus said, "and I will make you fishers of men." At once they left their nets and followed Him. *Mark 1:16–18*

Teaching aid: Colorful crepe paper streamers in rolls. Cut a three-foot length for each child to take home.

Gospel truth: Jesus helps us tell others the Good News of our salvation in Him.

Have you ever gone fishing? It's fun, but it sure takes patience. You find just the right spot. You cast your line into the water. *Pretend to do so.* And you wait, sitting very still. After a while, you pull your line back in and try again. Sometimes you get nothing. But sometimes you get a fish!

In our Gospel lesson today we hear that Jesus talked to Simon and Andrew. They were fishermen. They knew how to catch fish. But Jesus wanted them to be fishers of men, not fish! That meant that Jesus wanted them to tell other people about God so that they could become His children also. Right away Simon and Andrew laid down their fishing nets and followed Jesus. They learned how to live as God's children from listening to Jesus and watching Him. They became good fishers of men by telling others about His love for them.

Jesus helps us to be His fishers of men too. He wants us to tell other people about how He died for us and rose again so that we can be forgiven and live with Him in heaven. We can tell people about Jesus with our words. And we can show them Jesus' love with our actions. If we are kind to others, we are telling them that God's children are kind. If we help them, we are telling them that God's children are helpful. Let's give it a try.

I need a fisher of men. Who will be Jesus' helper? *Have the child stand near you. Give him one end of the streamer to hold.* Hold this pretend fishing line. Pick out a person near you. Tell him something about Jesus. *Offer a whispered hint such as "Jesus loves you" if necessary. Then unroll the streamer until it is long enough to reach that child. Tear off the end and let him hold the same piece as the helper.* Good fishing! Let's try again. *(To helper)* Pick another person here and tell that person something about Jesus. *Repeat the process three times until the helper is holding three streamers "attached" to three other children.* You're a great fisher of men! Thank you. *Take the streamers from the children.*

Sometimes the people you tell about Jesus will be excited to learn about Him, and sometimes it will seem as if they aren't. But don't give up. It's just like fishing. Ask Jesus to help you be patient and try again. Ask Him to send the Holy Spirit to help that person listen to your message and believe. Always be ready to tell people again and again. Our message is so happy and important that we want all people to hear it and believe it. God will help us and them.

I have a pretend fishing line for each of you to take home today. It will remind you that you can be Jesus' fishers of men. You can tell others about Him. You can show others that you are one of God's children. And the best part is that God will help you go fishing. He will help you be a good fisher of men.

Prayer: Dear Jesus, thank You for asking me to be one of Your fishers of men. Help me tell other people about Your love for them. Help me show people that I am a Christian—one of Your children. Please open their hearts to listen and learn about You. Amen.

The Most Amazing Teacher

<hr/>

FOURTH SUNDAY AFTER THE EPIPHANY: Mark 1:21–28

Text: Jesus went into the synagogue and began to teach. The people were amazed at His teaching, because He taught them as one who had authority. *Mark 1:21–22*

Teaching aids: Piece of chalk, small chalkboard, whistle, an alphabet book, and a Bible placed in a box or bag.

Gospel truth: God works through parents, teachers, pastors, and others to share the Good News of His salvation in Jesus.

I brought some tools with me today. These are tools that people use to do a job. Let's see if you can guess what that job is. *Show each of the teaching aids to the children except the Bible.* What is this? What is it used for? Who do you think would use all of these tools? *(A teacher.)* You learn many things from your teachers at school, don't you? They have studied a lot to learn the things they teach you. They know it's important that you get a good education.

Jesus was a teacher while He was here on earth. He taught the people how to live as God's chosen people. He told them about God's love for them. Sometimes He visited the synagogue, where He even taught the teachers who had studied God's Word for many years. The teachers were amazed that Jesus knew so much. He explained things that they had never known before. He even gave His own life on the cross to take the punishment for the sins of the people He taught. He was the most amazing teacher ever.

Now Jesus has returned to heaven. But He still teaches us. He gives us family members to tell us about God's love and how He sent Jesus to die for us. Who are the people at your house who tell you about Jesus? *(Let children respond—parents, grandparents, brothers, sisters.)* They learned about Jesus from studying a special book. What do you think that book is? *(Hold up the Bible.)* Yes, God's book, the Bible, contains true stories about God and His love for His people. It tells us that God still loves us, even though we have done wrong things. Jesus died to take away those sins. We are God's forgiven children.

Other people have studied God's Word, too, and taught you about Him. Can you think of some other people who tell you about Jesus? *(Pastor, Sunday school teachers, day school teachers, vacation Bible school teachers, friends, etc.)* That's right. Those helpers love Jesus so much that they want you to know about Him. They study the Bible to learn more about God, so they can share that good news with you. Many of those people are here today. They are gifts from God, aren't they? Without them we might not know about Jesus. Let's thank them now for teaching us about Him. Please stand with me and turn toward those helpers. *Look toward congregation.* Repeat these words with me: Thank you / for helping us learn / about our Savior, Jesus.

Now let's thank God for His Bible and His many helpers that teach us about His love. Let's pray together:

Prayer: Dear God, thank You for Your gift of the Bible. Thank You for our parents, grandparents, family members, pastor(s) *(name church workers the children know)*, for our Sunday school teachers, and others who teach us about You. Thank You for Jesus, the most amazing teacher. Help us to listen to them and learn more about You and Your love. Amen.

Prove It!

⟸◆⟹

THE TRANSFIGURATION OF OUR LORD:
Mark 9:2–9

Text: There He (Jesus) was transfigured before them. His clothes became dazzling white, … Then a cloud appeared and enveloped them, and a voice came from the cloud: "This is My Son, whom I love. Listen to Him!" *Mark 9:2–3, 7*

Teaching aid: Before beginning the talk ask a child to be your helper. Place a beach towel over his/her head so that only the child's arms and legs are showing. Lead the child to the group carefully.

Gospel truth: Jesus is truly God's Son, our Savior.

Can you guess who my helper is today? This is someone you know. Let's ask the helper some questions. How old are you? Do you have any brothers or sisters? What grade are you in at school? *(To the group)* Can anyone tell me who is under the towel? How did you know who it was? Did it help to hear his (her) voice? How can we see for sure who this is? How can my helper prove who he is? *(Take off the towel.)* Now we can really see who the helper is. *(Name)* proved who he is. When he took the towel off, we could see him much better.

Long ago Jesus told His helpers who He was. He showed them that He could make sick people well. He told them about His Father in heaven. Jesus explained that He would have to die and rise again to take away the sins of all people. The helpers knew a lot about Jesus, but they didn't know everything. In a way it was as if they couldn't see all of Jesus, just like we couldn't see all of *(child's name.)*

One day Jesus took three of His helpers, Peter, James, and John, with Him to a quiet place on a high mountain. There Jesus let His helpers see Him in all of His glory. Jesus' clothes became very, very bright. They were whiter than anyone could ever make them—even with bleach! Two men from heaven appeared and began talking with Jesus. A cloud appeared, and a voice from the cloud said, "This is My Son, whom I love. Listen to Him!"

Jesus' helpers were frightened by what they saw and heard, but they realized how very special Jesus was. He wasn't just a great man. Jesus was God's Son. God loved Him very much. It was God speaking from the cloud. He wanted the helpers to listen to what Jesus was saying. Jesus would be going back to heaven soon, and the helpers would be the ones to tell the good news of God's love to others. Jesus wanted to show them how very important their job would be. He wanted them to know that God would be with them and help them.

Jesus doesn't have to prove to us who He is. God's Holy Spirit helps us learn all about Him from the Bible. We know that He is God's Son and our Savior. We can tell friends the good news that God loves us and forgives our sins because of Jesus. God proved He loved us when He sent Jesus to die and rise for us. And we believe it!

Prayer: Dear Jesus, thank You for proving to Your friends that You really are God's Son and our Savior. Thank You for helping them spread the good news of God's forgiveness. Help us to share that message with our friends and family members, and with each other. Amen.

Just Say No!

FIRST SUNDAY IN LENT: Mark 1:12–15

Text: At once the Spirit sent Him out into the desert, and He was in the desert forty days, being tempted by Satan. He was with the wild animals, and angels attended Him. *Mark 1:12–13*

Teaching aid: A dish of M&M's; prepare an adult to help you, as indicated.

Gospel truth: God helps us say no to temptation and forgives us, because of Jesus, when we fail to do so.

Hold the dish of candy so that all of the children can see it. Look what I have. I love M&M's, especially the blue ones. M-m-m-m-m-m-m. I could eat this whole bowlful. Really. I love M&M's. But there's just one problem. These aren't my M&M's. They belong to my best friend, *(name)*. He (she) asked me to hold them for him. He's going to treat the children in his Sunday school class. It's a surprise from him. He should be coming any minute to get them. I promised not to eat them—just hold them.

Look at the candy. But—they sure look delicious. He probably wouldn't miss one or two, would he? I mean, there are plenty in the dish. And he probably won't have that many children in his class today. I could maybe eat one or two. He wouldn't even know. This is really tempting.

What do you think I should do? Should I keep my promise not to eat them? Or should I sneak one or two? *(Accept the children's ideas.)* Thank you for helping me. This temptation is just too much for me.

Do you know what temptation is? It means that you want to do something even though you know it's wrong. It's very hard to say no and not do that thing. I should say, "No, I'm not going to eat even one M&M. It's wrong to take something that belongs to someone else." But I'm still wishing I could eat these yummy you-know-whats.

Who is so powerful that He could help me say no to this temptation? That's right. Jesus could help me. And He does—many times each day. Every time I have trouble choosing the right thing to do, Jesus helps me make my decision. Every time I'm tempted to do wrong things, Jesus can help me say, "NO!" He knows what it's like to be tempted.

When Jesus lived here on earth, He went out into a desert without food or water. He became very hungry and thirsty. The devil tempted Jesus. He tried many times to get Jesus to obey him rather than God. But each time Jesus said no. Finally, the devil left Him.

So Jesus knows what it's like to see this scrumptious treat and want to eat it. And Jesus can help me say no. *Set the dish down next to you.* He can help each of you as well. When you are tempted to do something naughty, ask God to help you say no. And if you aren't able to say no, and you do something wrong, tell Jesus that you are sorry. He will forgive you and still love you. He died to take away our sins for us. He's our loving Savior.

Prayer: Dear Jesus, we know that You are powerful enough to say no to any temptation. Please help us say no when we are tempted. Please forgive us when we don't say no and do something wrong. Amen.

At this point the "friend" can enter to retrieve the candy. He (she) thanks you for not eating the treat. He offers you and each of the children three M&M's for being so honest.

What You See Is What You Get

SECOND SUNDAY IN LENT: Mark 8:31–38

Text: Then He (Jesus) called the crowd to Him along with His disciples and said: "If anyone would come after Me, he must deny himself and take up his cross and follow Me." *Mark 8:34*

Teaching aids: Rules discussed below printed on a sheet of paper; a baseball cap; a cross pin (one for each child, if possible).

Gospel truth: God helps us live as His children and follow Jesus' example.

I can see by looking at all of you that you are ready to learn more about Jesus. Right? We like to get together to do that. That's what this group does. People join many different groups for many different reasons. We can tell what they like by the things they do. I have a young friend named Josh. He's six years old. Some of his friends are starting a secret club. It's a group that does things together. *Hold up the rules.* Here is a list of their rules. Josh has asked me to help him decide if he should be in the club. Let's see.

Rule 1: You must wear your hat so everyone knows you are part of the club. *Put the cap on your head or a helper's.* Is that a good rule? Sounds okay to me too. That way everyone would know that Josh is part of that group. If people see the boys coming along the street, they would know that the boys are part of that club.

Rule 2: You can never play with anyone who is not part of our club. What! Is that a good idea? What if Josh wants to play with another friend at school? What if he gets invited to play at another boy's house? How would that make his other friends feel? Do you think this is the kind of group Josh should be part of? Do you think he'd be happy to be seen with this hat now? I don't think so either. *Take off the hat.*

If Josh obeyed the second rule, he wouldn't be following Jesus' example of loving others, would he? He would be hurting the feelings of his other friends. In the Gospel lesson today Jesus tells us: "If you want to be one of My followers, you need to take up your cross and follow Me." Does that mean that we have to die on a cross like Jesus did? No. Jesus already did that for us. He means that He will help us follow His example. Being a Christian means showing God's love to all people, not just some. Being a Christian means saying no to people who want us to do wrong things with them, even if they make fun of us for it. Being a Christian means asking God to help us make good decisions. Being a Christian means knowing God will help you through every trouble and hard time.

Sometimes it seems easy to be a Christian—like now, here at church with other Christians around us. But sometimes it's hard to be a Christian—like when your friends want you to tease and laugh at someone in school. It's hard to say no when the other children are saying bad words and want you to say them too. It's hard to be a Christian when the others make fun of you for going to church and Sunday school instead of going with them to a big hockey game.

We need some big help with this. Who can help us? Right! Jesus can help us to take up our cross and follow Him. These cross pins can help us remember that we are God's children. And when others see them, they will know that we are Christians. Jesus has promised to help us follow His example. Let's talk with Him now.

Prayer: Dear Jesus, we are happy to be Your followers. We want people to know that we love You. Help us to live as Christians each and every day. Help us make wise decisions as we follow Your example. Amen.

Jesus Clears the Temple

THIRD SUNDAY IN LENT: John 2:13–22

Text: When it was almost time for the Jewish Passover, Jesus went up to Jerusalem. In the temple courts He found men selling cattle, sheep, and doves, and others sitting at tables exchanging money. So He made a whip out of cords, and drove all from the temple area, both sheep and cattle; He scattered the coins of the money changers and overturned their tables. To those who sold doves He said, "Get these out of here! How dare you turn My Father's house into a market!" *John 2:13–16*

Teaching aid: Ask an adult to help you with the first part of the lesson.

Gospel truth: Jesus fulfilled the mosaic law and offered Himself to die as the perfect sacrifice for all sin.

When the children have been seated in their customary place, another adult enters the worship area and, in an authoritarian manner, demands that changes be made. (For example: "The pastor should stand over here instead of over there. Children, stand up! All children wearing shoes with shoelaces sit over here. I want the candle holders moved to another place.") After the changes have been made, the helper may leave.

What happened here? What did that man (or woman) do? *Allow children to respond.* Yes, he certainly gave a lot of orders, didn't he? And we all did exactly what he said. Why, he ordered us around as if he owned the church!

In today's Gospel lesson John tells how Jesus came into the temple in Jerusalem. Jesus saw men selling cattle, sheep, and doves. People were buying these animals to use for sacrifices to pay for their sins. Other men traded Jewish coins for the money travelers brought from their own countries. The visitors needed Jewish coins for the temple offering.

What Jesus saw made Him very angry. People were not using God's house in a loving way. Jesus made a whip and chased the animals away from the temple. He knocked over the tables of the money changers, and He ordered all of the merchants out of the temple. "How dare you turn My Father's house into a market!" He shouted. Why, Jesus acted as if He owned the temple!

"Wait a minute," the people said. "What gives You the right to do this? Who put You in charge, anyway? Prove to us that You have the authority to do what You just did."

Jesus could have called down thunder and lightning to prove that He was really God. Or He could have asked angels to appear and tell the people who He was. But instead He said, "Destroy this temple, and I will raise it again in three days." He didn't mean the temple church in which the people had come to pray and sacrifice. He meant the temple of His own body.

The Jews had come to the temple to offer animals to God as sacrifices, just as God had told them to do in the law He had given to Moses. When the animals were killed, God forgave the sins the people had done that year. Now Jesus had come to be the sacrifice for the sins of all people. Jesus would die on the cross, and God would forgive the sins of everyone who believed in Him. Animal sacrifices had to be made every year, but Jesus' sacrifice of His own body on the cross would last forever.

Jesus could act like He owned the temple because everything that went on in the temple pointed to Him. He was the best sacrifice, the one God accepted as complete payment for all our sins. Because Jesus died for us, we can go directly to God in prayer and worship.

Everything in our temple—our church—points to Jesus too. We come to hear His Word and to learn how He died for our sins. We pray in His name. We worship Him as our dear Lord and Savior.

Prayer: Forgive us, Lord, for letting anything interfere with our worship of You today. Help us listen, learn, and pray. We ask this in Jesus' name, for He died to pay for all our sins. Amen.

The Cure
for Snakebite

≈>◦<≈

FOURTH SUNDAY IN LENT: John 3:14–21

Text: Just as Moses lifted up the snake in the desert, so the
Son of Man must be lifted up, that everyone who believes
in Him may have eternal life. For God so loved the world
that He gave His one and only Son, that whoever believes
in Him shall not perish but have eternal life. For God did
not send His Son into the world to condemn the world,
but to save the world through Him. Whoever believes in
Him is not condemned, but whoever does not believe
stands condemned already because he has not believed
in the name of God's one and only Son. *John 3:14–18*

Teaching aids: Bottle with picture of Mr. Yuck (symbol for
poison), rubber snake, paper with the word *sin.*

Gospel truth: God sent His Son, Jesus, to save us from
death by the poison of sin.

Display bottle with poison symbol. Do you know what
this sign means? What does it say about what's in this bottle?
What will happen if you eat or drink what's in this bottle?
This sign means poison. If you eat or drink poison, you will
get very sick. You may even die.

Display rubber snake. Sometimes poison comes from
animals or plants. Some kinds of snakes are poisonous. What
would happen if a poisonous snake bit you? If the poison is
not removed right away, you will get very sick. You may even
die.

Long ago God led His people on a long journey through
the desert. The people complained about the food God had

given them. They didn't believe God could lead them safely to their homeland. God punished the people for not trusting Him by sending poisonous snakes. The snakes bit the grumbling people. The people became sick, and many died.

The people came to Moses and told him they were sorry they had complained. Moses prayed to God. Moses asked God to take away the poisonous snakes.

God loved His suffering people and sent a cure for snakebite. He told Moses to make a snake out of bronze and to lift the snake up on a tall pole. Then anyone bitten by a snake could look up at the bronze snake and live.

Display the word "sin." One poison is even worse than poisonous snakes or poisons that we might eat or drink. That poison is sin. Sin has poisoned everyone who has ever lived. It makes people sick—with meanness, selfishness, lying, fighting, and cheating. And it always leads to death. Doctors and paramedics cannot save us from this poison. No scientist has ever discovered a cure.

God hates sin. But He loves sinful people so much that He gave them the cure for sin's poison. He sent His Son, Jesus, to become a human being. God put all of the poison of people's sin on Jesus. Then He lifted Jesus high on a cross, just like the bronze snake in the desert. Jesus died on the cross to cure us from the poison of sin.

Jesus said, "God so loved the world that He gave His one and only Son, that whoever believes in Him shall not perish but have eternal life" (John 3:16). Instead of dying, Jesus says we will have eternal life, living forever with Him. And since sin's sickness doesn't control us, He will help us live as God's healthy children—treating each other with love, kindness, honesty, and fairness.

Prayer: Dear God, the poison of sin has made our lives sick. We see this sickness in the bad things we think and do and say. But You sent Your Son, Jesus, to die on the cross to cure us from sin's poison. Forgive us our sins, God, for Jesus' sake. Amen.

Life through Death

⋙◆⋘

FIFTH SUNDAY IN LENT: John 12:20–33

Text: Jesus replied, "The hour has come for the Son of Man to be glorified. I tell you the truth, unless a kernel of wheat falls to the ground and dies, it remains only a single seed. But if it dies, it produces many seeds. The man who loves his life will lose it, while the man who hates his life in this world will keep it for eternal life. Whoever serves Me must follow Me; and where I am, my servant also will be. My Father will honor the one who serves Me." *John 12:23–26*

Teaching aid: One raw peanut in the shell.

Gospel truth: Jesus willingly suffered and died on the cross to save sinners. Through Baptism, Christians also die to sin and rise to new life in Him.

This morning I've brought along something that is good to eat. *Display peanut in shell.* Do you know what this is? Yes, peanuts are very good to eat. I think I'll roast this peanut and eat it all by myself. Or maybe I'll save it to eat later on.

Oh, excuse me; I forgot my manners. I shouldn't talk about eating this peanut in front of you when I don't have enough to share. I wish I could turn this into enough peanuts for everyone. H-m-m-m. I have an idea.

Peanuts come from plants, don't they? I think these things grow on the roots of the plant. Let's open this shell and see what's inside. *Open shell and display peanuts.* What part of the peanut plant is this? What would I need to do to get lots more peanuts?

Yes, the nut we eat is actually the seed of the peanut plant. I could eat the nut or keep it in a safe place because it's special. But it might spoil, and it will be the only peanut I have. If I want lots of peanuts—enough to share with all of you—I must bury the seed in the ground.

Usually we bury things because they are dead. But only by burying the peanut seed will we get live peanut plants and lots and lots of peanuts. Saving the peanut too long really loses it; eventually it will rot and be no good to anyone. Burying it in the ground really saves it, giving us all the peanuts we'll ever need.

Jesus' disciples loved being with Him. They liked to travel from town to town, listening to Him tell about His Father's kingdom and watching Him make sick people well and blind people see. They would have liked to keep Him with them like this forever. But Jesus told them some disturbing news. He said, "The hour has come for the Son of Man to be glorified. I tell you the truth, unless a kernel of wheat falls to the ground and dies, it remains only a single seed. But if it dies, it produces many seeds" (John 12:23–24). Jesus wanted the disciples to know He was going to die very soon. This was God's plan to save them and all people from their sins.

Then He told them, "The man who loves his life will lose it, while the man who hates his life in this world will keep it for eternal life" (John 12:25). People who believe in Jesus are like seeds too. Because you are baptized, you share in everything Jesus did. He died, and so do you. The old you that liked to act mean and selfish, that liked to use bad words or hurt people, has been put to death and buried through your Baptism. Then Jesus rose from the dead. And a new you, someone who loves God most of all and who acts a lot more like Jesus, rises to a new life too—treating other people with love and kindness, the way Jesus would. And when we forget to act as Jesus would, He works in our hearts to make us say we're sorry.

Jesus promises that this new life will last forever and that we will always be with Him. "Where I am," said Jesus, "My servant also will be" (John 12:26).

Prayer: Dear Lord Jesus, You came to earth to suffer and die for my sins. I am sorry for the wrong things I have done, and I need Your forgiveness. Help me to love You most of all and to live the way You want me to live. In Your name I pray. Amen.

Why Jesus Had to Die

PALM SUNDAY: Mark 15:1–39

Text: It was the third hour when they crucified Him. The written notice of the charge against Him read: THE KING OF THE JEWS. They crucified two robbers with Him, one on His right and one on His left. Those who passed by hurled insults at Him, shaking their heads and saying, "So! You who are going to destroy the temple and build it in three days, come down from the cross and save Yourself!" In the same way the chief priests and the teachers of the law mocked Him among themselves. "He saved others," they said, "but He can't save Himself! Let this Christ, this King of Israel, come down now from the cross, that we may see and believe." Those crucified with Him also heaped insults on Him. *Mark 15:25–32*

Teaching aids: A wooden or cardboard cross, a small cross of heavy paper for each of the children.

Gospel truth: Jesus willingly gave His life on the cross for us, to save us from our sins.

Do you have a favorite television hero? We like to watch cartoons about superheroes because we like to see them use their super powers to get out of any tough situation they find themselves in. We even like to pretend we are superheroes with plenty of power for any emergency.

But everyone knows that superheroes on TV are make-believe. Real people have no super powers. Real people can't hold back a speeding car with one hand or stop a bullet with their fist. When real people fall off a tall building, they get hurt or even killed.

Only one real person—Jesus, the Son of God—was powerful enough to save Himself from any danger. Because He was God's Son, everything on earth and in heaven obeyed Him. He made blind people see and crippled people walk. He told the wind to stop blowing and the waves to calm down. He even made dead people come back to life.

Jesus' enemies hated Him. They wanted to make Him stop preaching and healing the people. They didn't want Him to raise any more dead people. So they arranged to have Him captured. At His trial they told lies about Him. Finally a Roman official said that Jesus would have to die.

Jesus' enemies took Him to a hill called Calvary. There they nailed His hands and feet to a cross. They stuck the bottom of the cross in a hole and left Jesus hanging there to die.

While Jesus was hanging on the cross, His enemies made fun of Him. "Come down from the cross and save Yourself!" they teased. "He saved others, but He can't save Himself!"

Do you think Jesus could have come down from the cross if He had wanted to? Of course He could. If He had wanted to, He could have called a thousand angels to come and kill the people making fun of Him. But Jesus just stayed there on that cross and died.

The cross was the reason Jesus had come into the world. "For God so loved the world," Jesus told Nicodemus, "that He gave His one and only Son, that whoever believes in Him shall not perish but have eternal life." God loved sinners, just like you and me—sinners who deserved to die for the wrong things they had done. He loved them so much He sent His Son, Jesus, to die in their place.

That love for us made Jesus want to stay on the cross, even though it hurt Him very much, even though He knew He would die. That's why the cross is so beautiful to everyone who believes in Jesus. It reminds us how much God loves us. It reminds us that our sins have all been paid for. For Jesus' sake we have been forgiven.

Here is a little cross to keep in your pocket. When you reach in your pocket and feel the cross, remember that Jesus died on a cross for you.

Prayer: Dear Lord Jesus, I'm sorry for all the wrong things I have done. Thank You for staying on the cross and dying for me. Amen.

The Egg Surprise

THE RESURRECTION OF OUR LORD:
Mark 16:1-8

Text: When the Sabbath was over, Mary Magdalene, Mary
the mother of James, and Salome bought spices so that
they might go to anoint Jesus' body. Very early on the
first day of the week, just after sunrise, they were on
their way to the tomb and they asked each other, "Who
will roll the stone away from the entrance of the tomb?"
But when they looked up, they saw that the stone, which
was very large, had been rolled away. *Mark 16:1-4*

Teaching aids: Three eggs—one hard-boiled, one broken
open and rinsed out, and one hard-boiled and decorated; a package of small foil-wrapped chocolate eggs or
jelly beans to share with the children.

Gospel truth: Jesus, who died on the cross for our sins,
rose victorious over sin, death, and the devil on Easter
morning. Because He died in our place, we will live eter-
nally with Him.

My friend Andy loved to watch plants and animals grow.
One day Andy's father brought home a plastic box with an
electrical cord attached to it. Through the clear sides of the
box Andy could see a light bulb and a thermometer.

"The box is called an incubator, Andy," Father said.
"We'll put this egg in the incubator." *Display first egg.* "You
must turn the egg over every morning and every night and
check to see if the temperature is still at the red line." Father
plugged in the electrical cord, and Andy saw the bulb light
up and felt how it began to warm the inside of the incubator.

Every morning and every evening Andy opened the incubator and turned the egg over. He checked the thermometer to make sure the temperature stayed the same. He made an X on the calendar each day to count how many days the egg had been in the incubator. But nothing happened to the egg. On the twentieth day Andy grumbled, "Nothing will ever happen to this dumb old egg. I like watching things that are alive. But this egg is as lifeless as a rock!"

On the twenty-first day Andy's mother said, "Hurry, Andy, and check the incubator. It's almost time to leave for church."

When Andy looked in the incubator, the first thing he saw made his mouth drop open in surprise. *Display empty egg shell.* "Oh, no!" he exclaimed. "It's not bad enough that nothing happened to my egg. Now it's broken! It's empty."

Just then Andy heard a peeping sound. He looked in the incubator again. Can you guess what he saw? That's right! He saw a little yellow chick, still wet from the inside of the egg. "Mom! Dad! Come and see!" shouted Andy. "I was afraid when I saw the egg was empty. But now I see that it's empty because the chick is alive. What a great Easter surprise!"

Dad helped Andy take care of the new baby chick. Then Andy's family went to church. Andy listened to the pastor read about three women who brought spices to the garden where Jesus was buried. When they got to Jesus' tomb, they found the stone was rolled away and the tomb was empty. An angel told them that Jesus had risen, but the frightened women ran away.

"I know just how those women felt," Andy told his parents after church. "It's just like when I found the eggshell. I was really scared. But when I saw the live chick, I was so happy."

"That's right, Andy," Mom said. "The empty tomb surprised and scared all of Jesus' friends. But when they found out He was alive, their fear turned to joy. Easter brings joy to us too. Because Jesus lives, we don't have to be afraid of death anymore. We will rise again like Jesus and live with Him in heaven."

That's why Easter eggs remind us of Jesus. *Display decorated egg.* The chick's new life makes us think about Jesus and the new life He won for us. *Distribute candy eggs to the children.*

Prayer: Alleluia! Jesus is alive! Alleluia! Amen.

Believing without Seeing

SECOND SUNDAY OF EASTER:
John 20:19–31

Text: Then Jesus told him, "Because you have seen Me, you have believed; blessed are those who have not seen and yet have believed." *John 20:29*

Teaching aid: An electric lamp.

Gospel truth: God's Holy Spirit gives us the faith to believe in Jesus as our Savior from sin.

Let's play a game together this morning. I'm going to tell you something, and I want you to decide whether you believe me or not. If you believe what I said, nod your head yes. If you don't believe me, say, "I doubt it." Do you all understand?

Are you ready? Here's the first one. "Many men and women are here in church today." *Pause.* I see you're nodding your heads. That means you believe what I said. How did you know? *Allow time to answer that they can see many people.*

You believed what I said because you could see many men and women in church. Let's try another one. "Today my robe and my stole are both white." *(Change as needed to describe what you are wearing.)* You believe me again, I see. Why did you believe?

How about one more. "A red fire truck is on its way down the center aisle." You say you doubt it? Why don't you believe? *Allow the children to explain that they don't see a fire truck.*

You have proven to me that you are willing to believe in things you see, but unwilling to believe in things you don't see. Most grownups follow that rule even more faithfully than children do. Yet there are some things that grownups and children believe even though they have never seen or understood them.

Show children the lamp. Can you tell me what will happen when I turn on this lamp? *Allow for response, then turn on lamp.* If you guessed that nothing would happen, you were right. Before the lamp will work, I must plug in the cord. Why does the lamp have to be plugged in? Yes, it needs electricity. But what is electricity? Can you tell me how it works?

My friend who is a scientist tells me that everything is made of tiny atoms so small that you cannot even see them. Each tiny atom has at least one proton, one neutron, and one electron. To make electricity, an electron from one atom moves to the next atom, while its electron moves to yet another atom. Millions of these electrons will be moving in this cord, and billions more in the wires in the church and outside on the utility poles.

Can you see any of these electrons? Of course not. Do you understand how this works? I know I don't. But I do believe the light bulb in this lamp will light up when I plug in the lamp and turn it on. *Turn on light.* If I didn't believe in electricity, I wouldn't be able to see where I'm going at night, or watch TV, or use my power tools.

After Jesus rose from the dead, His friend Thomas said he wouldn't believe Jesus was alive unless he saw Him for himself. Jesus came to Thomas, and Thomas believed. We haven't seen Jesus, but by the help of the Holy Spirit we know He died for us. We believe He rose from the dead, and we know He will come back to take us to heaven to be with Him. Not believing in Jesus would mean not knowing He is our Friend and Savior. Jesus said,

"Blessed are those who have not seen and yet have believed" (John 20:29).

Prayer: Jesus, You are our Savior and our Friend. Please give us Your Holy Spirit to keep our faith in You strong until we see You face to face. Amen.

Just Like They Said It Would Be

⟹◆⟸

THIRD SUNDAY OF EASTER: Luke 24:36–49

Text: He said to them, "This is what I told you while I was still with you: Everything must be fulfilled that is written about Me in the Law of Moses, the Prophets and the Psalms." Then He opened their minds so they could understand the Scriptures. He told them, "This is what is written: The Christ will suffer and rise from the dead on the third day, and repentance and forgiveness of sins will be preached in His name to all nations, beginning at Jerusalem." *Luke 24:44–47*

Teaching aids: A book, a toy, a pair of socks, three paper scrolls.

Gospel truth: Jesus is our crucified and risen Savior, as foretold by Scripture.

I would like to tell you about one of the nicest gifts I have ever received. Listen carefully so you will be able to identify the present I'm talking about.

One Christmas my parents gave me something I had wanted for a long time. The present had blue covers. Some words were written on the front cover. I keep the present on a shelf in my office and read it when I write the sermons for church. *Change the description to fit the book you're using.*

Now that you've heard about my favorite present, we'll find out how well you listened. Here are three presents that I received. *Display the toy, the book, and the socks.* Do you know which of these was my favorite present?

How did you know that I liked the book the best? What do you remember that I said about my present? *Allow time for the children to recall your description of the book.*

After Jesus died on the cross and rose again from the grave, He came to see His disciples. The disciples felt very confused. Why had Jesus died on the cross, they wondered. And what did it mean that now He was alive again?

Jesus knew His disciples were confused. He used God's Word to explain what had happened. "This is what is written," He told them, "the Christ will suffer and rise from the dead on the third day, and repentance and forgiveness of sins will be preached in His name to all nations, beginning in Jerusalem."

With Jesus' help, the disciples understood what He was telling them. They remembered what they had learned in the Law, the Prophets, and the Psalms. *Read from first scroll.* Moses wrote these words about Jesus centuries before He was born: "The Lord your God will raise up for you a prophet like me from among your own brothers. You must listen to him" (Deuteronomy 18:15). *Give first scroll to a child; read from second.* The prophet Isaiah described Jesus' suffering like this: "He was despised and rejected by men, a man of sorrows, and familiar with suffering … the punishment that brought us peace was upon him, and by his wounds we are healed" (Isaiah 53:3, 5b). The psalm writer told how Jesus' hands and feet would be pierced by the soldiers' swords and His clothes divided in a game of dice. The psalmist also wrote that God would make Jesus alive again: "You will not abandon me to the grave, nor will You let your Holy One see decay." (Psalm 16:10). *Distribute scrolls.*

"I get it!" Simon Peter might have shouted. "God sent our Friend, Jesus, to suffer and die on the cross for our sins."

"Of course!" James and John would have agreed. "And He rose again on the third day, just as the psalmist said He would." Jesus had helped His disciples understand that He was the Savior God had promised in His Word. And He gives us His Holy Spirit to help us believe that Good News too.

Prayer: Dear Lord Jesus, help us to recognize You as our Savior through the words of the Bible. Amen.

The "Pretty Good" Shepherd

———◆———

FOURTH SUNDAY OF EASTER:
John 10:11–18

Text: "I am the good Shepherd. The good Shepherd lays down His life for the sheep. The hired hand is not the shepherd who owns the sheep. So when he hears the wolf coming, he abandons the sheep and runs away. Then the wolf attacks the flock and scatters it. The man runs away because he is a hired hand and cares nothing for the sheep. I am the good Shepherd; … I lay down My life for the sheep." *John 10:11–15*

Teaching aids: A dishtowel and band to use for a shepherd's headdress; a stuffed toy lamb; a shepherd's crook or cane, if available.

Gospel truth: Like a good shepherd, Jesus laid down His own life to save those He loves.

I'm looking for someone who likes animals to do a job this morning. Who would like to be a shepherd and take care of this little lamb? *Choose one child.*

Shepherds in Jesus' day were hired to take care of flocks of sheep. They wore headdresses like this for protection from the hot sun. *Put dishtowel on child's head and secure with band or cord.* They used a staff with a crook on the end to rescue sheep who were in trouble. *Give staff to child.*

Let's pretend that you are taking care of your flock of sheep. *Give stuffed lamb to child.* You lead your sheep into a beautiful meadow full of tasty grass. What do you think a good shepherd would do? *Allow children to answer.* Yes, I'm sure the sheep will want to eat the tasty grass. You're a pretty good shepherd.

Now let's suppose the sheep have eaten all the grass they want. There is a stream with a quiet pool just a little ways ahead. You know the water in the pool is cool and sweet. What would a good shepherd do? *Allow children to answer.* The sheep will love drinking from the quiet pool of cool, sweet water. You really are a pretty good shepherd.

Now you're leading your sheep to a new pasture. On the way you must pass through a narrow valley with steep cliffs on both sides. You might be able to climb up these cliffs by yourself, but you certainly could not do it with a lamb in your arms. Just as you get to the narrowest part of the valley, you see two bright eyes lurking in the shadows and hear the growl of an enormous wolf. You're a pretty good shepherd, but this is an awful situation. If you put the lamb down so you can climb up the cliff, the wolf will eat it. But if you don't put the lamb down, the wolf is going to eat you! What would you do? *Allow children to answer.* I'm sure I would drop the sheep and climb if I were in your place. We may be pretty good shepherds, but shepherding is just a job, after all. It's not worth risking our lives.

Jesus said that each of us is like this little lamb. *Take lamb from child.* Jesus said, "I am the good Shepherd" (John 10:11). Jesus takes cares of us, making sure we have everything we need, just like the pretty good shepherd did. But Jesus said there is one very important difference. He said the pretty good shepherd was hired to take care of the sheep. When the wolf comes, the pretty good shepherd runs away. The sheep can't save themselves from the wolf, so they die. But we are sheep who belong to Jesus, the Good Shepherd. He lays down His life for His sheep. The Good Shepherd died so His sheep can live.

God's Holy Spirit helps us trust our Good Shepherd, Jesus. We know He died for us. We follow Him all through our lives with confidence, like sheep follow a good shepherd. And at the end of this life, we know that He will lead us home to be with Him forever in heaven.

Prayer: Jesus, You are the Good Shepherd who gave Your own life so we could live. Help us always to follow You, here on earth and when You call us home to be with You in heaven. Amen.

Of Vines and Fruit

———>·◇·<———

FIFTH SUNDAY OF EASTER: John 15:1–8

Text: "I am the vine; you are the branches. If a man remains in Me and I in him, he will bear much fruit; apart from Me you can do nothing." *John 15:5*

Teaching aids: The largest potted tomato plant available, scissors.

Gospel truth: Our relationship with Jesus is like that of branches to a vine. He provides all we need: forgiveness of sins, power to live a God-pleasing life, and the hope of everlasting life. Only through our relationship with Him can we bear fruit.

Spring always makes me eager to start my garden. I can't wait for the plants to grow and begin bearing fruit. Just thinking about my garden, I can almost taste the ripe red tomatoes and crunchy orange carrots.

Every spring I buy tomato plants like this and set them out in my garden. I carefully place each plant in a hole and cover the roots with soil. Each evening when I go home, I check my tomato plants. Sometimes I give them plant food or water. Other times I pull the weeds which have grown up around them. I watch for the little yellow flowers which show where the tomatoes will be. And I prop up the branches when the green tomatoes start to grow to make sure the branches won't break.

But this year I have a great idea. So that I won't have to go home to pick the tomatoes when they're ripe, I've decided to have them grow right here in my office at the church. *(Adapt to fit your situation.)* I'm going to snip off one of the branches of this tomato plant. *Cut off one branch of the plant.* I'll put the branch on my desk. I'll give it water and plant food when it needs it, and sit at my desk and watch the tomatoes ripen. Then when they're ready, I'll pick them and eat them right there.

I can see that some of you think this isn't a very good idea. Why won't my plan work? What will happen to the branch I cut off? *Make sure the children understand that the branch will die.* The branch can live only when it's connected to the vine. Without the life the branch gets from the vine, it will never bear fruit. It will only wither and die.

Jesus used a vine and branches to tell us how much we need to be connected to Him. He told His disciples, "I am the true vine, and My Father is the gardener" (John 15:1). God the Father planned for you and me, just as I planned for my garden. He looked forward to watching us grow and bear fruit. He made us part of the true Vine, His Son, Jesus. Through that true vine, He gives us everything we need—not just food and water, but also forgiveness, through Jesus' death on the cross, for all the wrong things we do.

Jesus said, "I am the vine; you are the branches. If a man remains in Me and I in him, he will bear much fruit; apart from Me you can do nothing" (John 15:5). Just like the little branch can't grow tomatoes when it isn't connected to the plant, so we can't do the things God wants us to do without the life and love we receive from Jesus. He gives us the power to live the way God wants us to live. Because we are connected to Jesus, we can bear fruit of the Spirit: love, joy, peace, patience, kindness, goodness, faithfulness, gentleness, self-control.

Being branches of Jesus, the true vine, means that we can talk to Him whenever we want. We tell Him we're sorry for the wrong things we've done and ask for forgiveness. We ask Him for whatever we need. We praise Him for being our Lord and Savior.

Prayer: Dear Lord Jesus, keep us connected to You, like branches to a vine, so that Your life in us will help us bear much fruit for You. We pray in Your name. Amen.

I Chose You

———◆◇◆———

SIXTH SUNDAY OF EASTER: John 15:9–17

Text: "You did not choose Me, but I chose you and appointed you to go and bear fruit—fruit that will last." *John 15:16*

Teaching aid: Before the beginning of the service, place a package of fruit drops candy somewhere slightly above an adult's reach.

Gospel truth: We are powerless to work out salvation for ourselves. But God has chosen us to be His own and redeemed us by the death of His Son, Jesus.

I'm going to need some help this morning. Just before church started, I noticed something that doesn't belong here. It almost looks like a package of candy. I tried to get it down, but it's just a little too high for me to reach. *Demonstrate that the candy is out of your reach.*

Is there anyone here who could reach that package for me? *Call on one of the older children.* You're pretty tall. Would you please stand up and try it? *Give child time to try.* No, I guess you're even shorter than I am. What if I let you choose another child to help you? You will have to pick up the child you choose so he or she can try to reach the package. *Allow child to choose a helper. Offer help as needed in lifting the chosen child up to try to reach the candy. Be sure the older child doesn't lift too much weight or get off-balance.*

Is there anyone else you could choose to help you reach the package? Yes, you may choose me if you want to. It looks like that would make us tall enough. Come pick me up, and I'll try to reach the candy. *Allow child to try.* You're right;

that will never work. I'm much too big for you to lift. If we want to reach that package, we'll have to go about it another way.

You couldn't reach the package by yourself. You couldn't reach it by choosing someone and lifting them up to get the package. So let's approach the problem another way. I will choose one of you. I will lift you up. *Choose one of the smaller children. Lift the child high enough to grab the package.*

Hooray! We have the package, and it's fruit drops! *Begin to distribute candy to the children. If very young children are present, you may want to just show the candy or give the candy to parents to supervise.* Oranges, cherries, limes, lemons ... this candy tastes like fresh fruit!

In today's Gospel lesson Jesus told His disciples, "You did not choose Me, but I chose you" (John 15:16). You couldn't reach the candy because you were too small. You weren't strong enough to pick me up to reach the candy for you. In the same way, we can't become God's children because we are sinners. The wrong things we do get between us and God, and we aren't powerful enough to get rid of them. But Jesus chose us. He obeyed God perfectly. Then He took away the sins that separated us from God by dying on the cross for them. Jesus chose us and made us God's children.

Jesus said, "I chose you and appointed you to ... bear fruit." By ourselves we can't do the things God wants us to do any more than we could reach that candy. But because Jesus chose us and made us His own, we can live His way and bear fruit for Him—fruit like love, joy, peace, patience, kindness, goodness, gentleness, and self-control. We can help people who need our help. We can get along with our brothers and sisters and obey our parents.

Jesus said God's fruit is better than oranges, limes, lemons, and cherries, because this fruit will last. Our joy in bearing fruit for Jesus lasts our whole lifetime here on earth and then forever with Him in heaven.

Prayer: Thank You, Jesus, for choosing us and making us Your children by dying for us. Help us to bear lots of fruit for You. In Your name we pray. Amen.

While I'm Away

———◆◆◆———

SEVENTH SUNDAY OF EASTER:
John 17:11b–19

Text: "I am coming to You now, but I say these things while I am still in the world, so that they may have the full measure of My joy within them. I have given them Your word and the world has hated them, for they are not of the world. … My prayer is not that You take them out of the world but that You protect them from the evil one. They are not of the world, even as I am not of it. Sanctify them by the truth; Your word is truth." *John 17:13–17*

Teaching aids: Tablet of paper, pencil, Bible.

Gospel truth: God's Word—which proclaims the Good News that Jesus died for us—is our sure defense against the dangers of Satan and the world.

Our Gospel lesson today comes from a long prayer that Jesus prayed the night before He died on the cross. Jesus knew exactly what was going to happen. He knew that He would die and then come back to life again. He knew that He would be with His disciples for a few more weeks and then go back to heaven to live with His heavenly Father.

Jesus also knew that the devil would try very hard to make His disciples forget all about Him and all He had taught them. He wanted to protect them from the devil's tricks. He wanted to keep them safe to do His work here on earth while He was gone.

Jesus' concern for His disciples was a bit like your parents' concern for you when they leave you home alone, or with a baby-sitter, for a little while. They want to be sure you will be safe while they are gone. They want to find you doing what you're supposed to be doing when they come back.

Pick up tablet and pencil and begin to write. "Don't let anyone in the house," your mother writes on a note for you and the baby-sitter. "Stay right here while we are gone," your father adds. "We'll be at Aunt Sarah's, and this is her phone number," Mother writes. "We'll be home at 6:30," adds Dad. "Don't tell anyone that we're not home. You may have some cookies and pop, but don't use the stove for anything. Call us at Aunt Sarah's if you have any problems at all."

Your parents write down their words so you can read them again while they are gone. If someone rings the doorbell, their words will remind you not to let them in. When you are hungry and want a snack, their words remind you to have some cookies instead of using the stove. Their words tell you where they will be and when they plan to return. And their words tell you how you and your baby-sitter can reach them if you need to talk to them.

When Jesus returned to heaven, He left God's Word to keep His disciples safe from the devil, who would tempt them to disobey Him. Jesus knew that would work—it's exactly what He had used when the devil tempted Him!

God's Word did protect the disciples when Jesus was gone. When their enemies tried to hurt and kill them as they had hurt and killed Jesus, they remembered how He had told them they would suffer for His sake but that He would always be with them. They boldly went out to all parts of the world to tell people about Jesus, just as He had told them to do.

Open Bible. When the devil tempts us to think that God doesn't love us, we can read again what Jesus said: "God so loved the world that He gave His one and only Son" (John 3:16). When the world makes money or having fun look too important, we remember that Jesus told us to love God most of all and love our neighbors as ourselves. We can read how

He said He would come again and take us to heaven to be with Him. And He even told us how to talk to Him in prayer when the devil makes us feel like we're all alone.

Prayer: Thank You, God, for giving us Your Word. Help us use it when the devil tempts us. Forgive our sins for the sake of Jesus, our Friend and Savior. Amen.

Living Water

THE DAY OF PENTECOST: John 7:37–39a

Text: "If anyone is thirsty, let him come to Me and drink. Whoever believes in Me, as the Scripture has said, streams of living water will flow from within him." By this He meant the Spirit, whom those who believed in Him were later to receive. *John 7:37b–39*

Teaching aids: Small paper cup for each child, a small canteen with just a few ounces of water, a large picnic jug filled with water, a dishpan or bucket to catch the overflow.

Gospel truth: The Holy Spirit works faith in the hearts of believers. The Spirit enables them to share this faith with others.

Have you ever gone for a long walk on a hot, sunny day? By the time you finished your walk, you were probably tired. You might have been hungry. But you definitely were thirsty! I'll bet you really wanted a drink of water.

Distribute paper cups. Here's a cup; doesn't that make you feel better? No? A cup without water does no good at all. Now you must feel more thirsty than ever.

Fill one or two cups from the canteen. Here's a tiny bit of water. Do you all feel better now? No, most of us didn't even get a sip, and now the water's gone. Even those who got a small drink can't get any more.

Today's Gospel lesson tells how Jesus stood up in a crowd one day and said, "If anyone is thirsty, let him come to Me and drink. Whoever believes in Me, as the Scripture has said, streams of living water will flow from within him" (John 7:37–38). I imagine that many people must have come to Jesus, carrying their cups and curious to see what kind of living water He was talking about.

But Jesus wasn't really talking about water that we can drink. He knew that the people who heard Him, like us, were really thirsty for God. They needed God the way thirsty people need water after a long, hot walk. Jesus said He would give them what they really thirsted for—the Holy Spirit. The Spirit would work faith in their hearts so they could believe in Jesus, their Savior.

Hold picnic jug over dishpan. The wonderful thing about the Holy Spirit—the living water Jesus was talking about—is that He will never be used up. *Refill the cups that had been filled from the canteen, then fill more cups.* There will be plenty for everyone who believes in Jesus. *Continue filling.*

The best thing about that living water—the Holy Spirit Jesus was talking about—is that it overflows. *Overfill a cup so that it overflows into the pan; direct one or more children to fill their cups from the overflow.* When the Holy Spirit fills us up with faith in Jesus, that faith shows in our lives. We can't help but talk about our Friend, Jesus, and what He has done for us. We treat everyone with kindness and love, just as Jesus treated us. We want everyone to know about our Savior.

When that happens, the Holy Spirit—that living water—bubbles up and overflows into the people around us, and they come to believe in Jesus, too, and to overflow into the lives of others.

Prayer: Holy Spirit, be our living water, filling us to the brim with faith in Jesus. Then help us to overflow, to show our friends and family with our words and lives what Jesus means to us, so that they may receive living water for their lives too. Amen.

Three Ways to See One Picture

——◆◇◆——

THE HOLY TRINITY: John 3:1–17

Text: For God so loved the world that He gave His one and only Son, that whoever believes in Him shall not perish but have eternal life. *John 3:16*

Teaching aids: On one side of a large piece of paper, draw a clock face reading 8:00. On the other side, draw three interlocking circles to signify the Trinity. For each child prepare a paper with the interlocking circle symbol. In the top circle print: "For God so loved _____." In the lower left circle print: "that He gave His one and only Son." In the lower right circle print: "that, believing in Him, _____ shall not perish but have eternal life." You will need a marker and a flat surface or an easel so you can draw on the large piece of paper.

Gospel truth: God the Father, who made us and all things, sent His Son, Jesus, into the world to save sinners. Through the power of the Holy Spirit we receive saving faith in Jesus.

Have you ever noticed that one picture may be used to tell several different stories? For example, take a look at this picture. *Show the clock.* What does this picture show? *Allow children to identify the clock; help them read the time, if necessary.*

When I look at this clock, I think of three different stories. I think about going to school in the morning when I was a boy. I always tried to leave the house before the clock said

8:00 so I wouldn't be late. This clock also makes me think of learning how to tell time. My father taught me how to count by five's to count the minutes after the hour on the clock. The third story is about the big clock we had in the hall when I was little. It had belonged to my grandparents, and now it belongs to me.

Reverse the paper to show the interlocking circles. This picture of three circles tells three stories about God. Each one is true and tells what God is like and what He does. But each one is different from the others.

Point to the top circle. God made the world and everything in it. *Draw a circle to signify the earth.* God the Father takes care of all that He made by providing rain and sunshine, food and shelter. *Draw a cloud and sun.* He made people, too, and gave them rules so they could live happily together with each other and with Him. *Draw some smiley faces.* When His people disobeyed Him, He wanted to save them and live happily with them again.

Point to the lower left circle. God sent His one and only Son, Jesus, into the world. Jesus, who is God, became a human being like you and me. When Jesus grew up, He died on a cross to pay for the sins of all people. *Draw a cross.*

Point to the lower right circle. Everyone who believes in Jesus will be saved and live with God forever. But we can't believe in Jesus by ourselves. God the Holy Spirit puts faith in Jesus in our hearts. He makes that faith grow like a strong, healthy plant. *Draw a plant.* He even makes that faith bloom in kind deeds that we do for each other because we love Jesus. *Draw flowers on the plant.*

In today's Gospel lesson, a man named Nicodemus came to Jesus to find out more about God. Jesus told Him all three of these stories. Jesus said, "God so loved the world *(point to top circle)* that He gave His one and only Son *(point to lower left circle)*, that whoever believes in Him *(point to lower right circle)* shall not perish but have eternal life" (John 3:16).

Through His Word Jesus tells those three stories to each

of us. *Distribute the individual papers to the children.* You can write your name on the blank line to finish the story. Jesus said, "God—that's God the Father—so loved Tracy or Ryan or Juan that He gave His one and only Son—that's Jesus—that, believing in Him—through the power of the Holy Spirit—you may not perish but have eternal life."

Prayer: God, You made us and loved us and sent Your Son to take away our sins. Help us to believe in You and live as Your children because of all that You have done for us. Amen.

Sundays Are Special

———◆———

SECOND SUNDAY AFTER PENTECOST:
Mark 2:23–28

Text: Then He said to them, "The Sabbath was made for man, not man for the Sabbath." *Mark 2:27*

Teaching aids: Sunday newspaper comic section, coffee cup, slippers.

Gospel truth: God rested on the seventh day of creation and awakened Jesus from the grave on a Sunday morning. He helps us to keep Sunday as a special day, a day when we can worship Him and rest.

Hold up Sunday comics. How many of you know what these are? *Wait for response.* That's right, they're the Sunday comics. It's fun to read them, isn't it? *Pick out a simple comic and read or tell about it.* Lots of people enjoy the Sunday comics. *Hold up coffee cup.* Here's another thing lots of grownups enjoy on Sundays, a nice hot cup of coffee. *Hold up slippers.* Some people like to sit in a comfortable chair with their robe and slippers on and drink a cup of coffee while they read the Sunday papers.

What are some other things that people do on Sunday? *Wait for a response regarding going to church and Sunday school.* That's right, many people go to church on Sunday. It's a special day we set aside to worship God, isn't it? In fact, it's the reason you're here today. When God made the world, He rested on the seventh day. He sent His Son, Jesus, to die in our place on Good Friday and then rise again on Easter Sunday morning. God helps us use Sunday as a day to gather together to tell Him how much we love Him, to sing songs about Him, and to listen to His Word. I'm glad you're here today so you can worship God.

How many of you go on picnics or to parties on Sundays? *Wait for response.* That's fun, isn't it? Lots of times my family and I like to *(fill in with an appropriate response such as go out to dinner, have friends over, watch TV, etc.)* after we get home from church and Sunday school. It feels good to relax with our families and friends on Sundays.

Do any of you know people who have to work on Sundays? *Wait for response.* Sometimes people have to work on Sundays, don't they? I'm sad when they can't worship with us on Sunday mornings. That's why we have Saturday evening and Monday evening services, so these people can worship too. *(Adapt to fit your situation.)* Do you ever do any work on Sundays? *Wait for responses and address them.*

In Bible days there were rules that said people *couldn't* work on the Sabbath—the day the people worshiped God. In fact, one day the disciples got in to trouble because they were picking kernels of wheat on the Sabbath. That's when Jesus said that the Sabbath, that's like our Sunday, was made for man, not man for the Sabbath. He wanted us to know that, yes, Sunday is a very important day. It's a day of resting and relaxing and worshiping Jesus, but it's more than a day of just laws and rules.

God wants us to enjoy our Sundays. He wants us to worship Him and remember the good news that Jesus rose from the grave on Easter Sunday morning. He also helps us honor Him by using His day for playing, or helping our parents, or just plain relaxing.

As you go home from church today, think of how you are going to honor God with the rest of your day. Then remember that God gave you this very special day because He loves you.

Prayer: Thank You, God, for the gift of Sundays. Thank You that we can worship You in church and Sunday school. Thank You for letting Your Son die for us and rise from the dead on Sunday. We pray in His name. Amen.

They're All Gone

<hr>

THIRD SUNDAY AFTER PENTECOST:
Mark 3:20–35

Text: I tell you the truth, all the sins and blasphemies of men will be forgiven them. *Mark 3:28*

Teaching aids: Chalkboard, or easel with a pad of paper; chalk or marker.

Gospel truth: Jesus forgives the sins of all repentant sinners.

How many of you try to be good? *Wait for response.* I'm sure your parents are very pleased when you try to be good, aren't they? I hope they tell you when you're good.

I try to do what's right, but sometimes, no matter how hard I try, I do wrong things. Sometimes I say something to my friends or my family, and it hurts their feelings. Sometimes I think bad thoughts about someone, and I know that's wrong. I remember once when I was your age I *(relate something you did as a child, possibly telling a lie or disobeying your parents, etc.).*

Those wrong things are called sins, and because we each do and say and think bad things, we're all called sinners. Today, we're going to make a list of sins. Then we're going to talk about what to do about those sins.

Label the list "Sins." I'm going to start the list with something I sometimes do. *Write down one sin such as "say bad things," "want what someone else wants," etc.* I feel bad about doing that, but if I'm really honest I have to admit I do it.

What else could be included on this list? *Wait for responses. Try to shorten the answers to one or two words each, such as "lie, cheat, hurt," etc.* Sometimes on the news we hear of bad things such as stealing or killing. *Add these to the list.* This list looks terrible, doesn't it?

Have you ever done any of these things? *Wait for response.* The Bible tells us that every single person on the earth is a sinner. In fact 1 John 1:8 says if we say we don't have any sins, we're fooling ourselves and not telling the truth.

That sounds pretty awful, doesn't it? What can be done about all our sins? *Wait for response, "Ask Jesus to forgive our sins." If no one offers it, ask, "What if we asked Jesus to forgive our sins?"*

What about asking Jesus to forgive us? Do you think He would be willing to do that? Suppose we prayed to Jesus and said, "Jesus, I'm really sorry I didn't obey my mom," or "Jesus, I'm really sorry I told a lie." Do you think Jesus would forgive us? *Wait for response.* Of course He will. There's another verse from the Bible that says this: "If we confess our sins, [God] is faithful and just and will forgive our sins."

That's exciting news! God tells us that because Jesus died in our place to take the punishment for our sins, He will forgive our sins, all of them. Let's take another look at the list of sins we wrote. What about this one? *For each sin ask, "Will God forgive this sin?" When the response is yes, erase or cross off the sin. If the children aren't sure, remind them God forgives all sins, because of Jesus, for those who are sorry.*

Remember that today's lesson had good news and bad news. The bad news is that we are all sinners, but the good news—and it's really good news—is that God forgives all our sins because of Jesus.

Prayer: Dear Jesus, please help me to do what I should. Help me remember that You forgive me when I do wrong, and that no sins are too big for You to forgive. Be with me today and always. Thank You, thank You, thank You for earning my forgiveness. Amen.

Starting Small

FOURTH SUNDAY AFTER PENTECOST:
Mark 4:26–34

Text: A man scatters seed on the ground. Night and day, whether he sleeps or gets up, the seed sprouts and grows, though he does not know how. *Mark 4:26B–27*

Teaching aids: Seeds, picture of grown plant from same type of seeds, trowel, watering can.

Gospel truth: God plants faith in our hearts and gives us His Spirit's power to help it grow as we study His Word and learn about Him.

This morning I brought some very tiny things to show you. *Put seeds in your hand and show the children.* What kind of seeds do you think they might be? *Wait for responses.* That's right, they're _____ seeds (*or tell what kind they are if no one guesses*).

I also brought along a picture to show you what they will look like when they are full-grown. *Show picture.* Imagine, those little tiny seeds will grow into a big plant like this. I don't understand how that happens, do you? All I know is that these tiny seeds will become big plants some day.

I brought along some things that I use when I want seeds to grow into big plants. *Bring out the trowel.* Here's a trowel. Maybe some of you have little shovels like this to dig with. When I want to plant the seeds I dig a little hole with this and put the seeds in the ground.

Bring out the watering can. Here's a watering can. When it rains a lot I don't need this, but if there isn't enough rain, I can water the seeds with this can.

But, you know, even though I put the seeds in the ground and water them, I still don't really understand how they grow. I just know they do, and I'm thankful for that.

There's something else that starts out very tiny and grows and grows. That something is our faith. *Point to baptismal font.* When we were baptized, God planted faith in us. We didn't look any different after we were baptized, and we probably didn't feel any different. Yet it was God's way of starting faith in us.

And you know what? Just like the tiny seeds, our faith doesn't stay small. God's Holy Spirit keeps our faith growing and growing, even though we might not understand why it's growing or how it's growing.

Can anyone think of ways God uses to help our faith grow? *Elicit responses such as learning about God's Word at Sunday school and church and learning Bible stories and songs about Jesus.* That's right. Every time we learn about Jesus, God's Holy Spirit makes our faith grow.

When you go home today, tell your family and friends that your faith is growing. God planted the faith in us, and He makes it grow through His Holy Spirit working in us.

Prayer: Thank You, dear God, for giving us faith and for making it grow in us. Help us want to read and study Your Word so Your Holy Spirit can make our faith grow stronger and bigger every day. Amen.

Powerful Water, More Powerful Jesus

FIFTH SUNDAY AFTER PENTECOST:
Mark 4:35–41

Text: He got up, rebuked the wind and said to the waves, "Quiet! Be still!" Then the wind died down and it was completely calm. *Mark 4:39*

Teaching aid: Jar, half-filled with water, with a lid.

Gospel truth: God is all-powerful and will protect us in time of danger.

Hold the jar of water on its side and rock it back and forth, making waves. I brought along a jar of water this morning. While I've been talking I've been doing something with this water. Who can tell us what I've been doing? *Wait for responses.* That's right. I've been rocking the jar back and forth, and that makes the water move around in the jar. But now I want the water to stop moving, so I'm going to tell it to stop. *Continue to move the jar so the waves continue.* Okay, water, stop moving. *Act surprised when it doesn't stop.*

Maybe the water didn't hear me. Maybe if we all told it to stop it would. Say with me, "Water, stop moving." *Have children say, "Water, stop moving."* That's funny. It didn't stop even when all of us told it to. Maybe we're not powerful enough.

Does anyone know how we can stop the water from moving? *Wait for responses.* That's right. If I hold the jar really still, the water will stop. Then I will have power over this water. *Hold the jar still and let the water stop.*

The only reason I was powerful enough to make this water stop was because I only had a little bit of water and because it was in a jar I could hold. The Bible tells us about a time when Jesus showed His power over a whole lake of water. *Read Mark 4:35–41.* What did Jesus do to make the water stop? *Wait for responses.* The disciples were surprised that Jesus even had power over things in nature.

Does Jesus still have power over things in nature? *Wait for responses.* He sure does. Jesus is God, and He can do anything. Why do you think that's important? *Lead the children to see that if in times of trouble God can do anything, then we can trust in Him to take care of us.*

There are lots of times when I'm afraid. Sometimes when I hear thunder and see lightning I get scared, or if someone I love is sick I get worried that he or she may not get better. It's at times like that when I'm glad I know that Jesus is always with me. All I have to do is pray to Him. I can say, "Jesus, You know I'm scared. Help me to not be afraid. Help me to trust that You are in control and You can make everything turn out for my good." Sometimes just talking to Jesus makes me stop being afraid. We know Jesus will protect us and take care of us, just like He took care of the disciples in our Bible reading today.

Prayer: Jesus, sometimes we are really afraid. Help us remember that You are in control. Help us remember that You will take care of us and protect us. Please be with us in times of trouble and let us feel You are there. In Your name we pray. Amen.

The Greatest Healing

——◆——

SIXTH SUNDAY AFTER PENTECOST:
Mark 5:24b–34

Text: Your faith has healed you. Go in peace and be freed from your suffering. *Mark 5:34*

Teaching aids: Band-Aids, medicine bottle, stethoscope, Bible.

Gospel truth: God is the greatest healer; through the life, suffering, and death of His Son, He heals us from the sickness of sin.

Today I brought some things to show you. I'm sure you'll recognize them right away, and I think you'll be able to tell what they're used for. *Bring out Band-Aids.* What are these? *Wait for response.* Sure, they're Band-Aids. What do people use them for? *Wait for response.* That's right. When you get a cut or a scratch you clean it off, then put a Band-Aid on to keep it clean and dry.

Bring out medicine bottle. Here's something else you'll recognize, I'm sure. It's a medicine bottle. Sometimes when you're sick your mom or dad will give you medicine. It's important to read the directions carefully so you only take the right amount and at the right time. This medicine will make you feel better, but you need to be very careful when you take it.

Here's something you might recognize too. *Take out stethoscope.* It's a stethoscope. The doctor uses it to listen to your heartbeat. He puts it on your chest. By listening to your heartbeat he can tell if you're sick or healthy. If you're sick, then he can figure out what to do to help you get better.

I have one more thing to show you. *Bring out Bible.* You probably all know this is a Bible. At first it might not seem as if it goes with these other things. They are all used to treat sicknesses or injuries. Does anyone have an idea how God's Word might fit with the other things I just showed you? *Wait for responses. Help children understand that God promises in His Word to always be with us and help us in times of trouble and sickness. He sent His Son, Jesus, to heal us from the sickness of sin.*

Each one of us has a sickness inside us called sin. Sometimes we say bad things to our friends or family. That's a sin. Sometimes we disobey our parents. That's a sin. Sometimes we tell a lie. That's a sin. No matter how hard we try, we can't stop sinning.

If we could only find a way to heal our sickness of sin we'd be all set, wouldn't we? Do you think any of these things I brought out could help us with our problem? *Wait for response.* The Bible tells us what to do about sin, doesn't it? The Bible tells us that Jesus died on the cross to take away all our sin. Just think about that! He took away all that terrible sin that's in us. Now when God the Father looks at us, He sees the love of Jesus and sees that we're all healthy.

You believe that Jesus died to take away your sin—that's what we call faith. Later on in the Bible reading, Jesus said a woman had such great faith that He healed her sickness and told her she wouldn't have to suffer any more.

When we believe in Jesus as our Savior, we don't have to worry about sin in us anymore either. Our sickness of sin is all gone, and we've been healed!

Prayer: Dear Jesus, You are the greatest healer. You healed us from the sickness of sin. Help us always to be thankful that You died and rose again for us. Now we know we can go to heaven to live with You when we die. Help us to tell others about You so they can be healed too. In Your name we pray. Amen.

The Best Blessing

<hr>

SEVENTH SUNDAY AFTER PENTECOST:
Mark 6:1–6

Text: Jesus said to them, "Only in his hometown, among his relatives and in his own house is a prophet without honor." *Mark 6:4*

Teaching aids: Two similar toys, one new toy, still in its packaging, one used.

Gospel truth: God showers us with blessings and helps us to recognize His blessings even when they're familiar to us and not new.

Have you ever walked through a toy store, looked at all the new toys, and wished you could have some? *Wait for response.* It's fun to look at new things, isn't it?

I brought along two toys to show you. Who can tell me the difference between them? *Wait for response about one being in a package and one not.* That's right. This one *(hold up packaged toy)* is new, and this one *(hold up second toy)* has been used.

When my children *(adapt to fit your circumstances, mention nieces and nephews, or neighbors, etc.)* were little, we sometimes would walk through the toy store at the mall. They would see all sorts of new things, and they would want them. Sometimes we'd buy a new toy, and then they'd be really excited.

But you know something? After the children had played with the new toy for a while, they would put it aside and go back to the old and familiar toys they had at home. In the store it looked like the greatest toy ever, but they soon realized their old, familiar toys were really what they wanted.

Listen while I read one of today's Bible readings to you. *Read Mark 6:1–6.* The people in Nazareth, Jesus' hometown, had known Jesus since He was a little boy. They remembered Him helping around the carpenter's shop and playing with the other boys and girls. Now when He was grown up, He came back to preach and teach to the people of Nazareth about God's love, and they didn't think He was very important. Just because Jesus was familiar to them, like this old toy *(hold up toy)*, the people thought He wasn't very valuable. They wanted a new prophet, just like children want a new toy *(hold up new toy)*, even though the old ones are still good.

Jesus knew the people didn't have faith in Him. The Bible says He didn't do any miracles there because of that. It's sad to think that Jesus' friends and neighbors missed out on His blessings because of their lack of faith.

God has given us lots of blessings, everything from toys, to food, to homes, to our families. He helps us to understand that just because a blessing isn't new, it doesn't mean we can't use it, enjoy it, and thank Him for it. As you go back to your homes today, pray with your family and thank God for all of His blessings—especially His greatest blessing—Jesus.

Prayer: Dear Heavenly Father, we thank You for all the blessings You have given us. Help us understand that all blessings come from You, and help us to be thankful for them. When we are tempted to forget about them, bring us closer to You and remind us of Your goodness. Thank You for Jesus, who is our biggest blessing. In His name we pray. Amen.

An Empty Suitcase

EIGHTH SUNDAY AFTER PENTECOST:
Mark 6:7–13

Text: Take nothing for the journey except a staff—no bread, no bag, no money in your belts. Wear sandals but not an extra tunic. *Mark 6:8–9*

Teaching aids: Small suitcase or satchel and a Bible.

Gospel truth: God provides everything we need. We don't need to worry about having "things."

Have you ever planned to go on a trip somewhere? *Wait for response.* One of the things you need to do is to pack your suitcase. I have a number of suitcases at home. Each one of them is a little bit different from the others. Some are large, for when I'm going to be gone a while, and some are small, for when I'll just be gone overnight, or for several days.

I brought along one of my small suitcases this morning. *Hold up suitcase.* Since it's not very big, I'd probably use it if I were just going somewhere for a day or two. What kinds of things would I put in my suitcase for a short trip? *Wait for responses. If no one brings up a jacket or extra money, mention them yourself.* It sounds like you're used to traveling.

I think you'll be surprised when you discover what I've packed in this suitcase, though. *Show the children that the suitcase is empty, except for a Bible.* It doesn't seem like I'm ready to go if that's all I packed, does it?

In our Bible lesson for today, Jesus sent His disciples out to preach the Good News about Himself. He sent them from town to town to tell people how much God loved them. He sent them out in pairs, two went to this city, two went to a different city, and so on. But here's the surprising part. Jesus told the disciples not to take anything for their trip except a walking stick. He specifically told them not to take extra clothes or money, or even an extra jacket. Where Jesus and the disciples lived, it was often cool at night, and they could have used the extra clothes to cover up, but Jesus said, "Don't take them."

It sounds unusual for Jesus to give directions like these. After all, the disciples were going to towns where they didn't know anyone. Where would they stay? What would they eat? Do you suppose the disciples were worried about those things? *Wait for responses.* I don't know exactly, but God's Word doesn't say the disciples argued with Jesus. They just went. They went from town to town, telling everyone about Jesus and His love.

The disciples knew that Jesus would take care of them. The Bible tells us that people gave the disciples food to eat and places to stay. They listened to what the disciples had to say, and lots of people became believers in Jesus.

Today, Jesus still wants us to tell others about God's love. He sends pastors and teachers and parents, and yes, even children, to tell others the Good News that Jesus loves them and died to pay the price for their sins. He continues to take care of the people who are doing the telling. He makes sure that each of us has clothes to wear, food to eat, a house to live in, and everything we need. He doesn't want us to worry about having things like that. We can depend on Him to care for us.

Prayer: Dear Jesus, thank You for providing me with everything I need. You make sure I have enough food, enough clothing, and a house to live in. You have even given me parents to guide and direct me. Help me always to do Your will. Help me remember that You will provide all I need. Most important, thank You for being my Savior and Friend. Amen.

The Time-Out Chair

NINTH SUNDAY AFTER PENTECOST:
Mark 6:30–34

Text: Then, because so many people were coming and going that they did not even have a chance to eat, He said to them, "Come with Me by yourselves to a quiet place and get some rest." *Mark 6:31*

Teaching aid: Small chair, set off by itself.

Gospel truth: God refreshes us with His loving care in Jesus.

Not too long ago I heard about a chair that is set off by itself, just like this one is. It's used in classrooms and sometimes in homes. It's called a time-out chair. Does anyone know what a time-out chair is for? *Wait for responses.* That's right. When someone breaks a rule, their teacher or parent tells them they have to sit in the time-out chair. Have any of you ever had to sit in a time-out chair? *Wait for responses.* How did you feel? *Wait for responses indicating loneliness, being separated, etc.*

Most children usually don't *choose* to sit in a time-out chair. It's usually a punishment, isn't it? What is supposed to happen while you're sitting there? *Wait for responses, indicating that you're supposed to think about what you've done wrong.* Sometimes if we're made to sit away from people, we rethink what we've done or said. Then Jesus can help us realize what we did was wrong and help us to say we're sorry. A time-out chair is used to help us so we don't do the bad thing again.

Our Bible verses today talk about a time when Jesus and

His disciples wanted to get away from everyone. In a way it was like using a time-out chair. It wasn't because they were bad, though. It was because they had been surrounded by so many people. Listen as I read from Mark 6:30–32. *Read verses.* The disciples wanted to go off where they could rest and be with Jesus. Maybe they needed to get their minds cleared up again after all the noise and crowds. They needed time to be alone so they could refocus on Jesus and His teaching. Maybe they just wanted to go off and pray.

But it didn't work exactly like they planned. Listen to what happened after they went off. *Read Mark 6:33–34.* The people followed them! At that point, Jesus had a choice to make, didn't He? He could have gone off to another place, or He could have stopped resting and started teaching the people again. You or I might have said to the people, "Go away. I'm resting and I want to be alone to think for a while." But that's not what Jesus did. The Bible says He had compassion on the people. That means He felt sorry for them. He knew they wanted to hear Him preach and teach about God's love, so that's what He did.

In this Bible lesson, Jesus shows us that it's good to go off by ourselves sometimes. It's good to take time to refocus on Jesus and His Word. Sometimes if you've been around people all the time, and you're tired of all the noise and confusion, it feels good to get off and just be alone. Jesus knows that's a good idea. Even He wanted to do that.

When we're by ourselves we can talk to Jesus about all the things we've said and done. We can refocus on our words and actions and ask ourselves if they were things that Jesus wants us to do and say. We can ask Him to help us share the love He gives us through the way we act.

Prayer: Dear God, thank You for parents and teachers who care about me and who want me to do the right thing. Help me see that time alone, whether I chose it or because someone chose it for me, can be very useful. Help me refocus on Your love for me. In Jesus' name I pray. Amen.

Never Too Small

TENTH SUNDAY AFTER PENTECOST:
John 6:1–15

Text: When Jesus looked up and saw a great crowd coming toward Him, He said to Philip, "Where shall we buy bread for these people to eat?" He asked this only to test him, for He already had in mind what He was going to do. *John 6:5–6*

Teaching aid: Small bag from a fast-food restaurant.

Gospel truth: Jesus can take what we have, say, or do and turn it into something great.

I eat breakfast early on Sunday mornings, and I'm sure some of you do the same thing. Since we've been here for a while, I thought I'd provide breakfast for the whole congregation this morning. That way nobody's stomach will growl during the sermon.

Bring out small food bag. This is what I brought to feed everyone. How do you think we should go about giving out this food to all the people? *Wait for response indicating there isn't nearly enough for everyone. Act surprised.*

You don't think there will be enough? What could we do? *Wait for response.* It would cost a lot to buy enough food for everyone here, wouldn't it?

This morning I'm going to read from a book of the Bible called John. Listen to what Jesus did when He ran into the same situation. *Read John 6:1–13.*

Did you hear what the little boy did in the story? *Wait for response: He gave Jesus the small amount of food he had.* How do you suppose that small amount of food was enough to feed all those people? *Wait for response. Jesus did a miracle and made more food.*

That's right. Jesus took the small amount of food that the little boy offered and made it be enough for everyone. In fact, when they finished there were more leftovers than what they started with. I'm sure the people were very surprised, aren't you?

Sometimes children think they can't do very much because they're small. Some of you are small, and yet you can do a lot! How many of you have jobs around the house? *Wait for response.* What are some of those jobs? *Wait for response.* Those are pretty important jobs, and I'm glad you do them.

But you have an even more important job, and that job is telling others about Jesus and His love. For this job, it doesn't matter whether you're big or small. You see, Jesus can take your words and actions and use them to do great things. Have you ever told someone about Jesus? *Wait for response.* What are some things you can do to help someone know about Jesus? *Wait for response, such as bringing others to church or Sunday school.*

Those are all important things that you can do. From now on, whenever you tell someone about Jesus, or do something to help someone, keep in mind that Jesus can use your small words or actions to do great things.

Prayer: Jesus, I know I'm not grown up yet. Sometimes people tell me I can't do much because I'm small. Help me to remember that by myself my words or actions might not be very big, but You can take them and do great things with them. Help me always want to do what I can to tell others about You, so they can know You love them too. In Your name I pray. Amen.

True Believers

≫◆≪

ELEVENTH SUNDAY AFTER PENTECOST:
John 6:24–35

Text: Jesus answered, "I tell you the truth, you are looking for Me, not because you saw miraculous signs but because you ate the loaves and had your fill. Do not work for food that spoils, but for food that endures to eternal life, which the Son of Man will give you." *John 6:26–27*

Teaching aids: Bag of candy, can of "unpopular" vegetables such as spinach or beets.

Gospel truth: God gives us the gift of eternal life through the death and resurrection of His Son.

Hold up can of vegetables. Who can tell me what this is? *Wait for response.* Sure, it's a can of _____. Since I like to share things with my friends, I'd be glad to share it with you. How many of you are my friends? *Wait for response.*

Hold up bag of candy. Who can tell me what this is? *Wait for response.* Sure, it's a bag of candy. Most children like candy, don't they? I could share it with all of you, couldn't I? Raise your hand if you think that would be a good idea. *Wait for response.* Usually I share my candy with my friends. How many of you are my friends? *Wait for response.*

I wonder if you noticed what happened? When I was holding up the _____, most of you didn't want that, so you weren't very anxious to be my friend. But when I was holding up the candy, more of you wanted to be my friend. Can anyone tell us why that was? *Wait for response that indicates they thought they might get candy, but they*

*didn't want the vegetables, so they didn't indicate friend-
ship.*

The same thing happened in Jesus' day. Many people followed Jesus because they thought they could get something
they wanted for their earthly life. Maybe they thought of Him
as a kind of magician who could do tricks and make good
things happen.

But many people missed the most important reason for
following Jesus. Jesus told people they could get to heaven
by believing He was the Savior. But some people were so
busy watching and waiting to see what Jesus could give
them for their earthly life, they missed that important message.

There are still people like that today. They are so inter-
ested in earthly things they forget about Jesus. Sometimes
when they get sick they come to Jesus and ask Him to make
them better, then they forget about Him. Later when they
need something again, they talk to Him again.

Jesus wants us to come to Him all the time. He wants us
to come to Him if we are sad or happy or hungry or filled up.
But most of all He wants us to come to Him, knowing we are
saved through His perfect life and His death on the cross. He
wants us to know we can come to Him in prayer any time
and for whatever reason. He wants us to know about His
love for us, how He died and rose for us, and how we can
know for sure we're going to heaven. That's the most important reason to come to Jesus.

Prayer: Dear Jesus, thank You for being our Friend. We
love You and want to be Your friend forever. Thank You for
letting us come to You all the time, any time. Help us to be
true believers who follow Your will. In Your name we pray.
Amen.

Better than Sandwiches

TWELFTH SUNDAY AFTER PENTECOST: John 6:41–51

Text: I am the bread of life. Your forefathers ate the manna in the desert, yet they died. But here is the bread that comes down from heaven, which a man may eat and not die. I am the living bread that came down from heaven. If anyone eats of this bread, he will live forever. This bread is My flesh, which I will give for the life of the world. *John 6:48–51*

Teaching aids: Loaf of bread, knife, peanut butter, and jelly.

Gospel truth: Jesus is the Bread of life who won forgiveness of sins and eternal life for us on the cross.

How many of you like sandwiches? *Wait for response.* What's your favorite kind of sandwich? *Wait for response.* I brought along some things that we can use to make a sandwich. *Hold up bread, peanut butter, jelly, and knife.* What kind of sandwich would I be able to make if I used these things? *Wait for response.* That's right. I could make a peanut butter and jelly sandwich. Who can tell me how to do it? *Wait for response.*

I'm sure lots of you have made sandwiches using things just like this, haven't you? My children (*adapt to fit your situation—nieces, nephews, neighbors, etc.*) have made lots of peanut butter and jelly sandwiches. Why is it that people make sandwiches? *Wait for response indicating that people eat to satisfy their hunger.* That's right. When you're hungry, a sandwich is easy to make, and it fills you up.

There's one thing that every sandwich needs, and that's bread. It wouldn't be much of a sandwich if all we used was peanut butter and jelly, would it? Besides, it'd be awfully messy.

Jesus talks about bread in the Bible. He says that people eat bread because they're hungry. That was true in Bible times, and it's true today. Bread, and other foods, fill us up, and for a while we're not hungry. But you know, a few hours later, we're hungry again. Then we need to eat again. We constantly need food for our life here on earth.

Without bread and other good food to eat, we would die. In our Gospel reading today, Jesus talks about a different kind of bread. Jesus says that He Himself is the Bread of life. Jesus is the one who won us new life with Him, and eternal life in heaven one day, by suffering and dying on the cross for us. He took all the punishment for all the sins that you and I have ever done. Now when God the Father looks at us, He sees the love and forgiveness of Jesus and says, "Come into heaven with Me. You can live with Me forever."

Anyone who eats bread on earth will get hungry again. Then they'll have to look for more bread. When God leads us to look to Jesus as our Savior, Jesus is all we need to live forever. We'll never have to look for more and more and more ways to get to heaven. We need to eat food for our earthly life, but Jesus is the Bread of life who gives us heavenly life.

Prayer: Dear Jesus, thank You for the gift of heaven. Thank You for telling us that You are everything we need to go to heaven. Remind us daily that You are our Savior. Keep us strong in our faith until the end of our life here on earth, then welcome us with open arms as we enter heaven. In Your name we pray. Amen.

Party Time

—————❯◆❮—————

THIRTEENTH SUNDAY AFTER PENTECOST:
John 6:51–58

Text: Just as the living Father sent Me and I live because of
the Father, so the one who feeds on Me will live because
of Me. *John 6:57*

Teaching aids: Party hats, noisemakers, balloons, and other
party decorations.

Gospel truth: Because Jesus died for us and rose again, we
will live with Him in heaven. That's reason to celebrate.

This morning I'm going to have some of you wear some
hats and hold some special things. These things will give
everyone clues about what we're going to be talking about.
*Put party hats on some children. Have others hold the
noisemakers, etc.* Now, think where you've seen some of
these things before. What do you think we're going to talk
about this morning? *Wait for the response that we're going
to talk about parties.*

That's right, we're going to talk about parties. What are
some reasons for people to have parties? *Wait for responses.* That's right. We might have a party for someone's birthday, or a graduation, or their wedding, or some other special occasion. People have parties because they want to
celebrate something. They want others to share their hap-
piness.

Does anyone know what we're celebrating today? *Wait
for responses.* We're celebrating because Jesus came from
heaven and suffered and died for us. We're celebrating that
Jesus gave up His life for us, and then rose from the dead. Do

you think that's an important reason to celebrate? *Wait for response.*

I think so too. Do you remember how we celebrated Jesus' birth at Christmastime? That was the beginning of the celebration. Later we celebrated Good Friday. Who remembers what happened that day? *Wait for response.* "Celebrate" seems like a strange word to use when we think about Jesus dying on the cross, doesn't it? But it's good news that Jesus was willing to give His life to pay for our sins. And then came Easter! That was an exciting celebration because we knew that Jesus rose from the dead. A few weeks later we celebrated Ascension, when Jesus went back to heaven to get our homes ready.

But there's even more to celebrate! Jesus said that all who believe in Him as their Savior will go to heaven with Him when they die. That's what we celebrate every Sunday. We celebrate because Jesus rose on Easter Sunday and gives us new life every day.

Now, we usually don't wear party hats when we go to church, do we? But there are some things that we do and say in church that remind us of a party. How many of you have seen your moms and dads go to the Lord's Supper? That's when they come to the front of the church and are given a little piece of bread and some wine. Jesus tells us that this is His body and blood, which He gave up for us when He died on the cross. That's one way the adults are celebrating. Some day you'll be able to do that special celebrating too.

Parties usually involve gifts, don't they? Can anyone think of a gift that you get in church? *Wait for responses.* Those are good ideas. God gives us many gifts in church—the forgiveness of our sins, the Good News that Jesus came to save us, the blessing that God will be with us as we leave the church and help us in everything we do.

The next time you're at a party, think about how we celebrate Jesus and His love for us. Think of how He died and then rose again so that each of us can have a home in heaven. That's a big reason to celebrate!

Prayer: Dear Jesus, thank You for giving us a huge reason to celebrate. We love You and are happy that we can go to heaven to live with You forever. Help us share that wonderful news with everyone we know, so they can celebrate too. In Your name we pray. Amen.

Only One Way

FOURTEENTH SUNDAY AFTER
PENTECOST: John 6:60–69

Text: Lord, to whom shall we go? You have the words of eternal life. We believe and know that You are the Holy One of God. *John 6:68–69*

Teaching aids: Small box tied tightly with lots of string; small box secured tightly with many layers of tape; small locked box.

Gospel truth: God gives us one answer to solve the problem of how to get to heaven—the life and death of His Son for our sins.

This morning I brought along several containers. Each one is a little different, but each one presents a problem. Here's the first one. *Hold up the box tied with string.* Why might we have a problem getting this box open? *Wait for a response that the box is tied with string.* You're right. There's a lot of string on this box. *Hand the box to a small child.* Would you like to try to get this box open? *Let the child try for a minute, but then acknowledge that it's pretty hard.* It would be very hard to get this box open by yourself, wouldn't it? Who knows how we could help get this box open? *Wait for responses—we could cut the string with scissors or a knife, untie all the knots, etc.*

You're right. We could get the box open if we had the right things to use. Here's another box. *Hold up the box wrapped with a lot of tape.* Who would like to try to open this box? *Hand the box to a small child. Let the child try for a minute, but then acknowledge it also is pretty hard.* By yourself, it would be hard to get this box open, wouldn't it?

Who knows what we could do to get it open? *Wait for responses—we could cut the tape with a scissors or a knife, tear it, etc.*

You're right again. We could get into this box by trying different things. Here's a third box. *Hold up the box that is locked.* It doesn't have string or tape on it. It should be easier to open. *Hand the box to a small child.* Would you open this for us? *Let the child admit he/she doesn't have a key, and the box is locked.* What if I had the key to that box? Could we open it then? *Wait for positive response.* If we didn't have a key, we could call a locksmith to open it, or we could maybe use a hammer and break it open. So there are a couple of ways to open even a locked box.

So far we had three boxes. Each one looked like it was going to be hard to open; yet for each one we figured out several ways to try opening it.

Some people say it's hard to get into heaven. They say you have to be very, very good and then maybe, if you're good enough, you can go to heaven. Some people even say there are *lots* of ways to get to heaven. They say if you try hard to be good, or if you go to church every Sunday, or if you pray a lot, then God will let you come into heaven.

But that's not right. There's only one way to get to heaven. Only one! In our Bible reading today the disciples say that Jesus is the only way to get into heaven. They knew that Jesus was the Savior of the world, and anyone who believed in Him would be saved. They knew you couldn't find any other way to heaven. Peter said to Jesus, "You have the words of eternal life."

Let's thank Jesus for opening heaven for us. Repeat the words of our prayer after me.

Prayer: Lord Jesus, You have the words of eternal life. Thank You for showing us the one way to get to heaven. Thank You for promising to take us to heaven with You. We are Your children. Amen.

You Can't Lie to Jesus

<hr>

FIFTEENTH SUNDAY AFTER PENTECOST:
Mark 7:1–8, 14–15, 21–23

Text: He replied, "Isaiah was right when he prophesied about you hypocrites; as it is written: 'These people honor Me with their lips, but their hearts are far from Me. They worship Me in vain; their teachings are but rules taught by men.' " *Mark 7:6–7*

Teaching aids: A large paper bag and a picture of Jesus.

Gospel truth: God gives us life in Jesus and helps us to honor Him with our whole heart.

Hold up the paper bag. Guess what! I have a real live kangaroo in this bag. If I open the bag, it will hop out and jump all around. What do you think about that? *Encourage the children to talk about the kangaroo in the bag. See if they buy the story.* So you don't think that there is a real kangaroo in this bag? *Open the bag.*

You were right! Of course there wasn't a kangaroo in here. Could a real kangaroo fit in this bag? No! That really was a lie that I told you. Do you know what it means to tell a lie? *Allow enough time to see if the children do understand about telling a lie.* Telling a lie means saying something that isn't true. It was not good of me to try and fool you by telling you a lie about the kangaroo in the bag. I did it so I could explain something to you.

In our Bible reading today, Jesus knew some people were not being truthful. They tried to talk and act as if they loved God, but they didn't understand God's love and share it with others. They tried to fool Jesus, like I tried to fool you with the kangaroo story. But God knew the people did not love Him with all their hearts. Jesus told the people they could not fool God.

I really do have something in the bag, but it's not a kangaroo. I won't lie to you again. Let's look in the bag and see what really is inside. *Pull out the picture of Jesus.* Who is this? It's Jesus! I put a picture of Jesus in the bag to remind you that Jesus loves you so much, He gave His life for you. He will help you to love Him with your whole heart and to share His love with others. He will help you to tell others the truth about Him, and He will even forgive you if you tell a lie.

Prayer: Dear God, please help us not to lie to You or to anyone. Help us to tell the truth even when it is hard to do so. And help us to tell everyone the one true way to get to heaven. We love you Jesus. Amen.

Good Job, Jesus

SIXTEENTH SUNDAY AFTER PENTECOST: Mark 7:31–37

Text: People were overwhelmed with amazement. "He has done everything well," they said. "He even makes the deaf hear and the mute speak." *Mark 7:37*

Teaching aid: A piece of paper resembling a young child's homework sheet. Print words such as "Good job, you wrote this story well" or "Good job, this is a beautiful picture" on it.

Gospel truth: God does all things well—including sending His Son as the perfect plan for our salvation.

Hold up the piece of paper and show it to the children. This is some homework that a child I know did. The teacher wrote these words on the paper, "Good job, you wrote this story well!" The teacher liked what this child did and told her so. What have you done well that someone liked very much? *Give the children time to answer the question.* What are some other things that you can do well? I can *(name some things that you can do. Then add to the children's list).*

We can do many things well. God helps us do these things. He gave us our hands so we can paint and write. He gave us our brains to help us think and learn.

But there are some things we cannot do. Our Bible reading tells us that people brought a man who could not hear or speak to Jesus, and Jesus made him well! I cannot do that. I cannot make anyone hear or speak. You cannot make anyone hear or speak. Only Jesus can do miracles. And there's something else only Jesus could do. Only Jesus, God's Son, could come to earth and live a perfect life and then die on the cross to pay for the things that we don't do well.

Read Mark 7:37 to the children. God's Word tells us that Jesus can do everything well. We're happy that Jesus did a perfect job in living, dying, and rising again for us. Good job, Jesus! Let's thank Jesus for His love.

Prayer: Thank You, Jesus, for loving us in such a perfect way. Take away the wrong we do. Be with us as we work and play and help us do all things as well as we can. Amen.

Follow Jesus

SEVENTEENTH SUNDAY AFTER PENTECOST: Mark 8:27–35

Text: Then He called the crowd to Him along with His disciples and said: "If anyone would come after Me, he must deny himself and take up his cross and follow Me." *Mark 8:34*

Teaching aid: None.

Gospel truth: God loves and forgives us through His Son and helps us to follow Jesus' loving example.

Ask the children to stand and do as you do, copying some simple actions. Put your hands on top of your head. Everyone do as I do. Do you all have your hands on top of your head? Good.

Now do this. *Clap your hands.* Good. You are following me very well. *Touch your toes.* What good followers you are! *Swing your arms.* You follow me well. *Sit down on the floor. Look to see if everyone is sitting.* What good followers you are. You followed me and did everything that I did. You can follow well.

Jesus told His friends, the disciples, and some other people to follow Him. He wanted them to share God's love with one another. He told them that following Him wouldn't always be easy, but He would help them to do it.

Jesus tells us to follow Him too. What are some ways we can follow Jesus and share His love? *Help the children understand that obeying Mom and Dad and following school rules are ways of living out our love for Jesus. Sharing Jesus' love with someone who is hurting is a good way to follow Him.* You are thinking of good ways to follow Jesus.

We like to follow Jesus' way because He loves us so much. But sometimes we forget and hit a friend, or talk in school when we're not supposed to, or *(name some other rules that the children mentioned)*. Jesus forgives us when we forget to follow Him. He loves us so much that He died on the cross to take the punishment for the wrong things that we do. Let's thank Jesus for being such a good leader. Let's ask Him to help us follow Him.

Prayer: Dear Jesus, You are a great leader. Help us to follow You and live as Your children. Forgive us when we do wrong. Thank You for loving us and helping us in every trouble. We love You. Amen.

Who Is the Best?

EIGHTEENTH SUNDAY AFTER PENTECOST: Mark 9:30–37

Text: He took a little child and had him stand among them. Taking him in His arms, He said to them, "Whoever welcomes one of these little children in My name welcomes Me; and whoever welcomes Me does not welcome Me but the one who sent Me." *Mark 9:36–37*

Teaching aid: None.

Gospel truth: God loves all people, regardless of age, and sent His Son to be their Savior.

Choose some children who are of different heights and ages. Help the children line up according to height, tallest to shortest. Let's make a long line with the tallest over here *(indicate where)* and the shortest over here *(indicate where)*. Some children are tall and some are short. *Ask the ages of some of the lined-up children.* Some children are younger than others and some are older.

Whom does God love the best? The youngest children? The tallest children? *Give the children time to answer.* Maybe God loves the shortest children best. No? You are right. God loves ALL the children just the same. *Ask the children to be seated.*

One day some of Jesus' friends asked Him who was the greatest. Whom did Jesus love the best? Jesus asked a little child to stand in the middle of His disciples and said, "Love Me like this little child loves Me." Children are special to Jesus. He knows that you love Him, even though you have never seen Him. That's because God's Holy Spirit put faith in your hearts when you were baptized. Jesus told grown-up people that they should have a simple loving faith in Him as you do.

Remember that you are special to Jesus and that He loves you very much. He loves each and every one of you the same, no matter how tall you are or how old you are. Everyone is the best with Jesus.

Prayer: Dear Jesus, thank You for loving me just the way I am. Always be with me wherever I go. I love You, Jesus. Amen.

God Doesn't Use Locks

——————◆——————

NINETEENTH SUNDAY AFTER PENTECOST: Mark 9:38–50

Text: For whoever is not against us is for us. I tell you the truth, anyone who gives you a cup of water in My name because you belong to Christ will certainly not lose his reward. *Mark 9:40–41*

Teaching aids: A box with a lock, or a small piece of luggage with a lock that can be locked and then opened with either a key or combination; a heart—cut from paper, a heart-shaped pillow, any item shaped like a heart.

Gospel truth: God helps us share His love in Jesus with others.

Put the heart-shaped object in the box or piece of luggage and lock it. I have something that I want to show you. It's really very pretty, and it was a special gift a friend gave me. I just need to get it out of this box (suitcase). *Try to open the box.* I can't get the gift out. This box is locked. I am really sad. I wanted to share my gift with you and now I can't. Does anyone know what I should do?

Give the children time to answer, "Open the lock." That's a great idea. I have the key right here. *Open the box and pull out the heart.* Look at my gift. What is it? *Let children respond.* My friend gave me this heart because she (he) loves me.

God loves me too. But He doesn't keep His love locked in a box. His love is always out in the open, right where I need it. God is always ready to love and forgive me. God does not use locks. I can always go to God with any problem. Nothing can keep me from Him.

God loves you too. He loves you so much He sent His only Son to die for you, to pay the price for your sins. You can go to Him with any problem. How do you ask God for help? *Help the children to understand that we can take every need to God in prayer.* That's right, we go to God by praying to Him and asking Him to help us.

God loves us so much, nothing—not even locks—can keep us from Him and His love. His love will spill over into our hearts and help us to love one another.

Prayer: Dear God, I am so happy that I can always come to You and talk to You. You make me happy with Your love. Thank You God for loving me. In Jesus' name. Amen.

Let the Children Come

TWENTIETH SUNDAY AFTER PENTECOST: Mark 10:2–16

Text: When Jesus saw this, He was indignant. He said to them, "Let the little children come to Me, and do not hinder them, for the kingdom of God belongs to such as these." *Mark 10:14*

Teaching aids: Glue or tape a picture of Jesus on a red paper heart. Cut another heart of the same size. Punch a hole in each heart. Fasten the blank heart with yarn or a paper fastener as a cover over the picture of Jesus.

Gospel truth: God loves all people and encourages people to love Him with the simple trust of little children.

Hold up the blank heart. Do not let the children see the picture of Jesus. When I see a heart I think of love. I know some people who love me very much. *Name some people who love you.* Who are some of the people that love you? *Give the children time to name several.* I know someone else who loves you. *Open the heart "book" to the picture of Jesus.* Who is this? Of course, it's Jesus.

Jesus loves all people. I know a story from the Bible about Jesus and some big people who wanted to keep some children away from Him.

One day some moms were bringing their children to see Jesus. They came to a place where Jesus was talking to a lot of big people. The moms brought the children nearer to Jesus. Jesus' friends said, "Go away. Jesus is too busy for little children." But Jesus said, "Let the children come to Me." And He hugged them and talked to them.

Jesus wanted the children to come to Him. He said that it is good for big people to love Him in a simple, trusting way like little children do.

Hold up the heart with the picture of Jesus. This heart reminds us that Jesus always loves us. We, big people and little people, are important to Jesus. We are so important to Jesus that He died on the cross for us to take away all the wrong that we do. Remember, Jesus loves you, and He'll always keep you close to Him.

Prayer: Dear Jesus, we are glad that You always have time for us. Thank You for loving us. Forgive the wrong that we do. We love You. Amen.

Jesus Is Better than Money

TWENTY-FIRST SUNDAY AFTER PENTECOST: Mark 10:17–27

Text: Jesus looked around and said to His disciples, "How hard it is for the rich to enter the kingdom of God." *Mark 10:23*

Teaching aids: In a large sack place some toys; an item that you value such as a piece of jewelry, a music box, a tool, or tickets to a sports event; and a picture of Jesus.

Gospel truth: God gives us His Son as our most precious gift.

Display the sack and pull out the item that you especially value. This _____ is very precious to me. I love it very much. *Talk more about the item and how much it means to you.*

Show the children the toys. Do you have some toys that you like a lot? What are they? Why are they important to you? *Give the children an opportunity to answer the questions.* What if someone asked you to give all these things away. How would you feel? What would you do? *Explore the children's answers. Then tell the following story.*

One day a very rich man came to Jesus and asked Him how he could get to heaven. Jesus told him to give away everything he had. The man loved all of his things more than he loved Jesus. He did not want to give everything away.

God loves us so much, He gave us His most precious gift—the life of His own Son, Jesus. When we think of God's great love, He helps us to love Him more than *(name some of the items that the children mentioned earlier, make sure to name the special item you value)*. We can play with our toys and love our favorite things, but first we remember the great love Jesus showed us in dying on the cross for us.

Prayer: Dear Jesus, You are the most important person in our lives. Help us to always remember You first. Thank You for loving us. We love You. Amen.

Does Jesus Love Best?

TWENTY-SECOND SUNDAY AFTER PENTECOST: Mark 10:35–45

Text: For even the Son of Man did not come to be served, but to serve and give His life as a ransom for many. *Mark 10:45*

Teaching aids: Two pictures of cars that are different colors and makes.

Gospel truth: God loves us unconditionally in Jesus.

I need to buy a new car, and I can't decide which car to choose. I have a great idea. You can help me choose which is best. *Hold up one picture of a car.* Do you like this one? I like the color. But what about this car? Do you like it? *Hold up the picture of the other car.* I like this one also. But which one is best? *Hold up both pictures.* Which one shall I buy? *Have the children vote by holding up their hands or clapping for the best one as you hold up each picture of the car.*

I think you chose this car. *Show the children the car that got the most votes.* One day James and John, two of Jesus' friends, asked Jesus which one of them was the best. What do you think Jesus told them? *Give the children time to answer.* That's right, Jesus loved both of them the same. It's not like choosing a car that we love best. *Hold up the picture of the car the children chose.* Jesus loves all people just the same.

Jesus explained to His disciples that God's children don't worry about who is best. They ask God to help them love and serve one another. Sometimes we don't act our best. Sometimes we do things that are wrong. We do not obey our parents, or we don't pick up our toys. Perhaps we hit a friend. But Jesus still loves us. He died on the cross to take the punishment for the wrong things that we do. Jesus loves us all the time, even when we do wrong. That is the kind of love only God can give.

Jesus is our example in serving and loving one another. Jesus fed hungry people and helps us serve people who need food and other things. Jesus helped people who were sick and lost in their sin and helps us love our friends who are sad and need to know about Him. Let's ask Jesus to help us serve one another today.

Prayer: Dear Jesus, forgive us for all the wrongs that we have done. Help us to remember to share Your love with our family and friends. Help us serve people who are hurting, just like You would. Thank You for loving us always. We love You. Amen.

No Busy Signals for Jesus

---⪢◈⪡---

TWENTY-THIRD SUNDAY AFTER PENTECOST: Mark 10:46–52

Text: Many rebuked him and told him to be quiet, but he shouted all the more, "Son of David, have mercy on me." *Mark 10:48*

Teaching aids: A telephone (a real one would be best, but a toy one will do); a small tablet or piece of paper and a pencil.

Gospel truth: Jesus loves us and will always listen to us. He is never too busy.

Pick up the phone and dial a number, listen, and then put the receiver back down. The line is busy. Someone is talking on the other end of the phone. *Wait a few moments and redial.* The line is still busy. I can't talk to my friend until the line is free.

This reminds me of a story in God's Word. Bartimaeus was a man who could not see. He was sitting along the side of the road. When Jesus walked down the road, Bartimaeus began to shout, "Jesus, Jesus!" The people told Bartimaeus to be quiet. But he shouted all the louder. Jesus stopped and talked to Bartimaeus. Jesus loved Bartimaeus. He listened to him and helped him to see.

Jesus will listen to us when we talk to Him. He always has time to listen to us when we pray to Him. Jesus' line is never busy like this telephone line. *Hold up the phone.* Sometimes people do not have time to listen to us. They might even tell us to be quiet, like the people told Barti-maeus to be quiet. But Jesus will never tell us to be quiet. He will always listen to us. He is always ready to help us with our problems.

We can pray to Jesus about many things. We can ask Him to help us, and we can tell Him how much we love Him. Jesus likes to hear us praise Him with songs and prayers. What would you like to talk to Jesus about? *Give the children an opportunity to answer. You might write down some of the ideas and include them in the prayer at the end of the talk.*

Jesus loves us so much that He is never too busy for us. Let's talk to Jesus right now. I have written down some of the things that you want to ask or tell Him.

Prayer: *Include the items listed by the children in your prayer. You might want to name the children that made the requests.* Dear Jesus, we know You have time to listen to us. We love You, Lord Jesus. Amen.

Loving God with Our Whole Heart

⇒•◆•⇐

TWENTY-FOURTH SUNDAY AFTER PENTECOST: Mark 12:28–34

Text: "Love the Lord your God with all your heart and with all your soul and with all your mind and with all your strength." *Mark 12:30*

Teaching aids: An old shirt ripped down the middle so it is not wearable, a large (about 12″ long) red paper heart.

Gospel truth: God gave His "all" for us in sacrificing the life of His Son; He motivates us to love Him with our whole heart.

Try to put on one half of the shirt. Put the other half aside or in a container so that the children cannot see it. Oh, dear, something is wrong with this shirt. There is only half of it. I can't wear half of a shirt. What do I need? *Give the children an opportunity to answer the question. Bring out the rest of the shirt. Put on the other half.* Now I can wear it. I need both sides to make it whole. If I were home I could sew the pieces together to make a whole shirt.

Fold the paper heart in half lengthwise and hold it up so that the children can see it. Look at this! It is only half of a heart! What do I need? *Help the children to answer, "A whole heart." When they do, open up the heart to make a whole one.* A whole heart is better than a half of one.

Fold the heart in half again and then open it. God asks us to love Him with a whole heart. By ourselves, we could not do it. We could not even love Him halfway. But God gave us the most wonderful gift in the world—the gift of His Son to die in our place. When we think of that great love, God helps us to love Him in return.

Many times when we play a game we try our hardest and give our all to the game. That is what God helps us to do. In His Word, God says "Love the Lord your God with all your heart." AND WE DO! Because Jesus loved us first. Let's tell Jesus how much we love Him.

Prayer: Dear Jesus, we love You with all that we have. We give You our whole heart because You gave Your whole life for us. Amen.

Go and Tell

⟫◆⟪

THIRD-LAST SUNDAY IN THE CHURCH YEAR: Mark 13:1–13

Text: And the Gospel must first be preached to all nations. *Mark 13:10*

Teaching aid: Funnel phones—Two plastic funnels (kitchen type) and a piece of plastic tubing.

Gospel truth: God sent His Son to be the Savior of the world; He empowers us to tell all the world that Good News.

Push the small end of each funnel into one end of the plastic tube. Talk into one funnel while someone listens at the other end. Choose a child and talk to her/him using the funnel phones. Jesus loves you. Did you hear what I said to you through the phone? Give the end of the phone to a friend. *Talk to another child.* Jesus loves you. *Continue this way with a few more children.*

God tells us in the Bible, "And the Gospel must ... be preached to all nations." God sent His Son, Jesus, to be the Savior of the world. God asks us to be His helpers and tell people that Jesus died on the cross for us. I guess we need more than our funnel phones to do that.

Whom could we tell about Jesus? *Encourage the older children to answer.* We can tell our friends "Jesus loves you." You can tell your baby-sitter, your aunts and uncles, and maybe your grandma and grandpa about Jesus' love.

How can we tell people who aren't close by about Jesus? *Encourage the children to answer.* We could write a letter or send a card with the words "Jesus loves you." We could telephone a friend. We could give our offering to help missionaries in their work of preaching the good news about Jesus.

There are many people who need to hear the good news about Jesus' love. When you leave here today, try to tell one person, "Jesus loves you." Jesus will help you do it!

Prayer: Dear Jesus, help us to tell other people about You. Thank You for loving us. Amen.

God Never Changes

SECOND-LAST SUNDAY IN THE CHURCH YEAR: Mark 13:24–31

Text: Heaven and earth will pass away, but My words will never pass away. *Mark 13:31*

Teaching aids: A clear colorless glass container (a large glass will work) filled with water; blue and yellow food coloring. If you do not have food coloring, use liquid tempera paint; use any two colors that combine to make a third color.

Gospel truth: Other things may change, but God never changes. His Word is always with us.

Show the children the container filled with water. Drop or pour some food coloring or paint into the water. What happened to the water? *Encourage the children to answer.*

Accept that answer and say. It changed colors. It was clear. It didn't have any color, and now it is blue *(whatever color). Add some yellow color to the blue.* Now what happened? It changed again! Now the water is another color.

Some things change. Leaves change color in the fall. We can paint our house and change the color. What else changes? *Give the children time to think and answer. Remind them that they change and grow up.* You change too. You once were a baby, but now you are bigger. We change many things every day. We change what we eat. We change what we wear. Sometimes I wear a suit, and sometimes I wear a jacket or shorts.

Things change. You and I change. But God never changes. He always stays the same. God always takes away the wrong that we do. He always forgives us. Jesus died on the cross for our sins because He loves us. And He always loves us. His love never changes.

God gives us the Bible, His Word. In Mark 13:31 God tells us: "But My words will never pass away." That means the forgiveness and salvation that God gives us in Jesus will never, never go away. His Word, the Bible will always be here so that we can read it. We can always hear and read about God's love.

God will never change. He will always love us and be near us.

Prayer: We are so happy to know that You will never change, God. Forgive us for all the wrong that we do. Thank You for Your Word. Thank You for always loving us. In Jesus' name. Amen.

Be Watchful

LAST SUNDAY IN THE CHURCH YEAR:
Mark 13:32–37

Text: What I say to you, I say to everyone, "Watch!" *Mark 13:37*

Teaching aid: A pair of binoculars or a small telescope.

Gospel truth: Jesus died to pay the price for our sin. One day He will return to take us to our home in heaven.

Look through the binoculars. I'm watching some people with these binoculars. I can see things up close with them. They help me watch better. Would you like to look through my binoculars? *Help several children to look through the binoculars. Give them a focus point. Very young children might not be able to see anything through them.* What did you see? Could you watch better and see closer with these than with just your eyes? Of course!

Do you think if I keep looking through these binoculars I will be able to see Jesus return and take us to heaven. *Let children respond.* You're right, probably not. No one knows when Jesus will return. And when He does, it will be a pretty big celebration, and we'll all know it.

Jesus loves us and helps us watch for Him. We share the great love He gives us with one another. We learn about Jesus and study His Word. We pray to Him and treat other people as we want to be treated.

Jesus tells us to watch and be ready for Him to return and take us to heaven. We are ready. We believe that Jesus died to pay the price for our sins. We know that we will live in heaven with Him one day. *Lay binoculars aside.* We don't need to look at the sky with binoculars to be ready for Jesus to return. We keep our eyes on the cross, knowing that Jesus died for us and will one day return to take us to heaven.

Prayer: Dear Jesus, watch over us all the time. Help us to listen to You and do what You would like us to do. Forgive us all our wrongs. Thank You for loving us. Amen.